# SKETCH: PUBLIC BUILDINGS

## How Architects Conceive Public Buildings

# SKETCH: PUBLIC BUILDINGS
## How Architects Conceive Public Buildings

LOFT

Editor and texts: Cristina Paredes

Art director: Mireia Casanovas Soley

Graphic design and layout: Anabel Naranjo

Translation: Lynda Trevitt/Equipo de Edición

Editorial project:

**2009 © LOFT Publications**
Via Laietana, 32, 4.º, of. 92
08003 Barcelona, Spain
Tel.: +34 932 688 088
Fax: +34 932 687 073
loft@loftpublications.com
www.loftpublications.com

ISBN: 978-84-96936-32-4

Printed in China

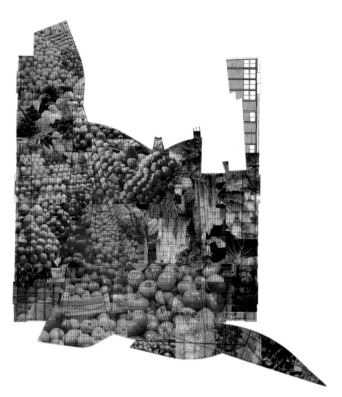

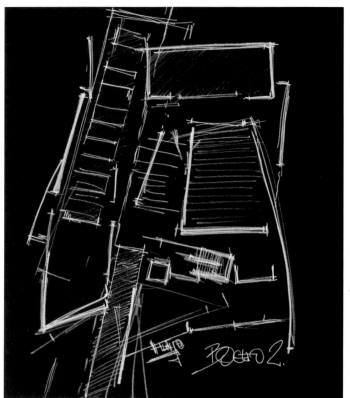

# Introduction

■ In architecture, a sketch is considered to be a drawing that describes a diagram or a general note of a project to be built. On the one hand, it is an artistic expression – the representation of a personal and original viewpoint about something. On the other hand, sketches of architectural designs reflect the architect's idea – a concept that has to be made into something real and physical. What adds importance to architectural sketches is the relationship established between two forms of creation: drawing and architecture.

Public buildings are constructions designed to provide specific services to a population: they may be schools, museums, theaters, hospitals, etc. They have a very important social, political and cultural value and their architecture not only has to be functional and adapt to the needs of each case, but should represent these values, too.

Architects use sketches as a tool for approaching their projects, to begin to give shape to the image they have in their heads. They also make it possible to show the architect's personality, lending them significant value. Each sketch is different and may involve a coarse, quick outline; an extremely simple, almost abstract, illustration; or drawings done in color. But whatever the material and support used to make an architectural sketch, the aim is always to record the most significant features of each building.

This volume not only demonstrates the importance of the sketch as a work of art and idea in itself, but also shows the whole of the creative process through to the end result. The following pages explore the phase that begins with the sketch, goes on to include models and renderings and eventually reaches the final plans prior to building.

# Patel Taylor

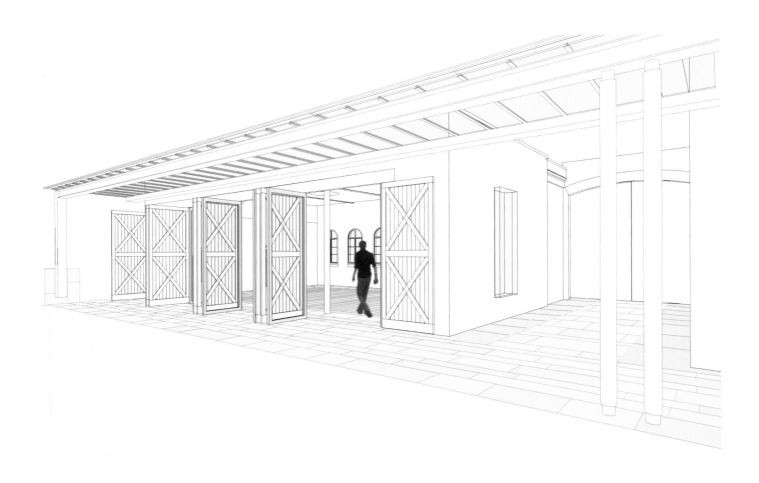

## Orleans House Gallery Twickenham, United Kingdom

■ Orleans House is the leading art gallery in the district of Richmond upon Thames. The architectural complex includes diverse buildings, such as an octagonal baroque hall designed by the architect James Gibbs, and an exhibition space that houses up to five temporary exhibitions a year. The old coach-house buildings and stables that have not been used in decades are being converted into new accommodation for a groundbreaking education program. The new site includes an educational area, offices, bathrooms and additional storage facilities. The areas are connected via a glass roof which provides homogeneity to the complex. The courtyard is expected to be used regularly as an extension of the education area.

9

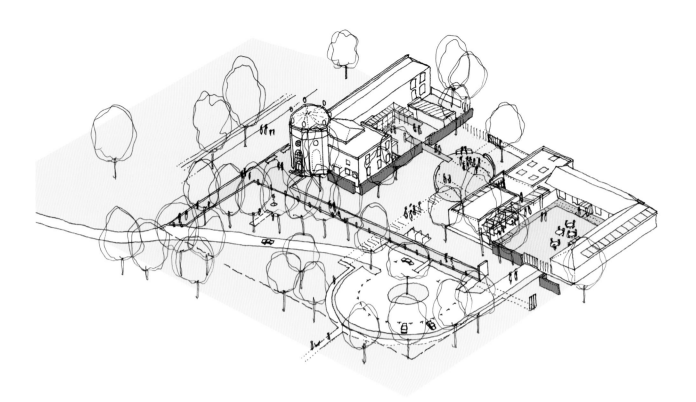

Sketches

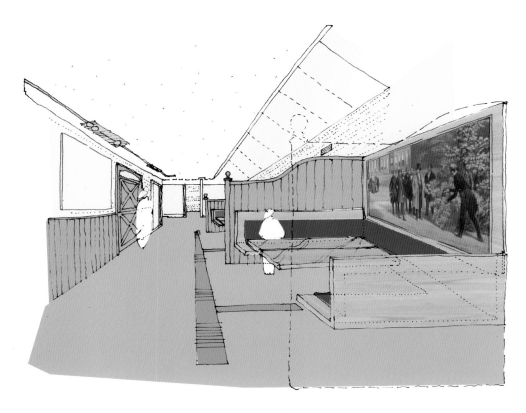

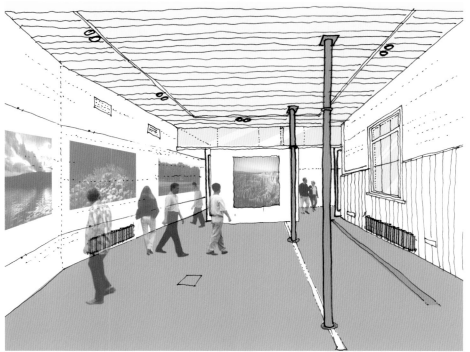

Sketches

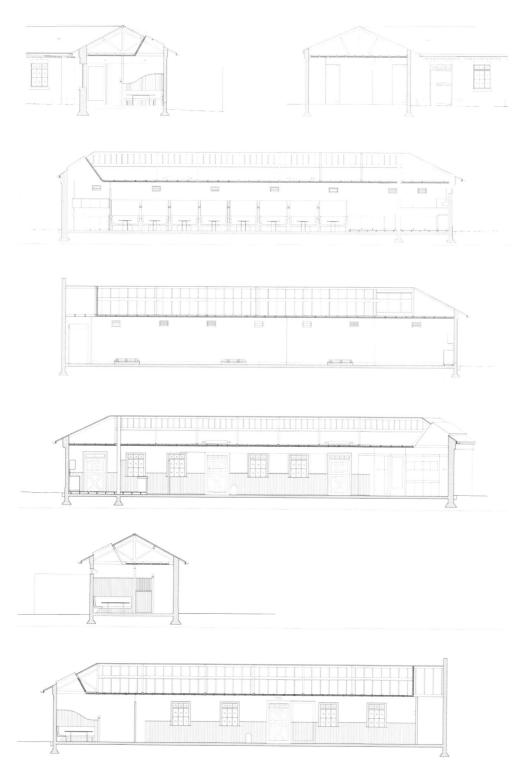

Sections of the stables building

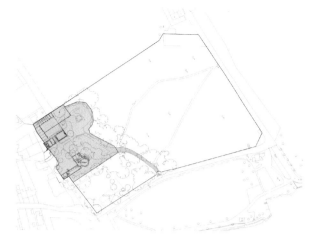

Location map

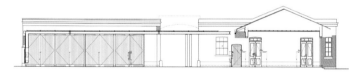

Elevation of the coach-house building

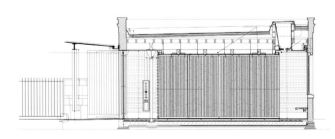

Section of the coach-house building

The collaboration between Pankaj Patel and Andrew Taylor, which quickly gained a reputation following their success in numerous international competitions, led to the foundation of the studio in London in 1989. Since then, it has grown into a medium-sized enterprise, big enough to handle most projects and at the same time small enough to uphold a consistent quality. It has a fairly mixed client portfolio, ranging from local governments to companies with private-sector interests. The architectural competitions and numerous awards they have won and the publications in which they have featured speak to the quality of their work.

**Patel Taylor**

# Lehrer Architects

## Bat Yahm Temple Newport Beach, CA, USA

■ The Bat Yahm Temple is located in Newport Beach, a coastal region with a temperate climate. The buildings are completely bathed in the pristine light of the environment. In the new synagogue, a square mass on top of the large, diaphanous chapel symbolizes Jacob's Ladder. The various elements are understood as a whole and are inter-related. Even the parking lot, with extensive grassy areas, plays the double function of car park plus children's playground. The building's sustainability is another significant feature and includes lighting control, natural ventilation and a water-capture system, and the grounds are planted with indigenous plants. The temple involved the creation of a place of worship for the Jewish community, a place where sustainability and beauty would become the principle of spiritual and aesthetic life.

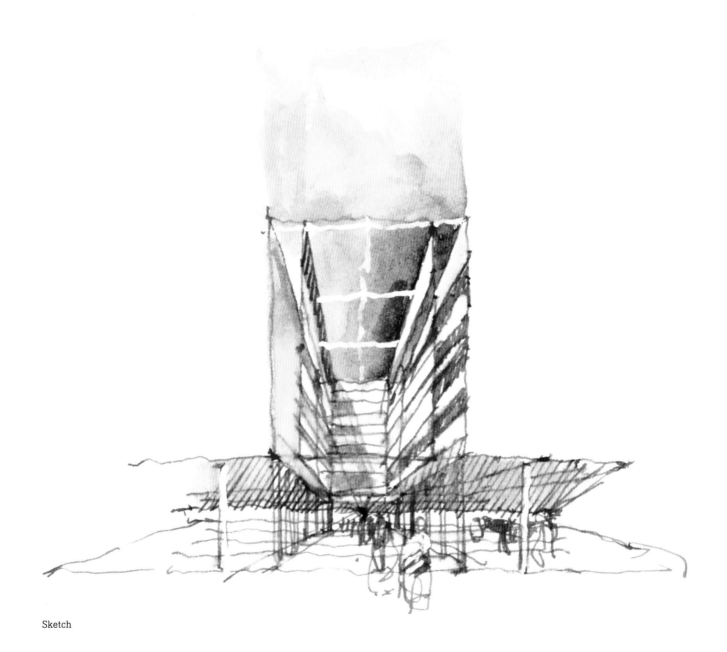

Sketch

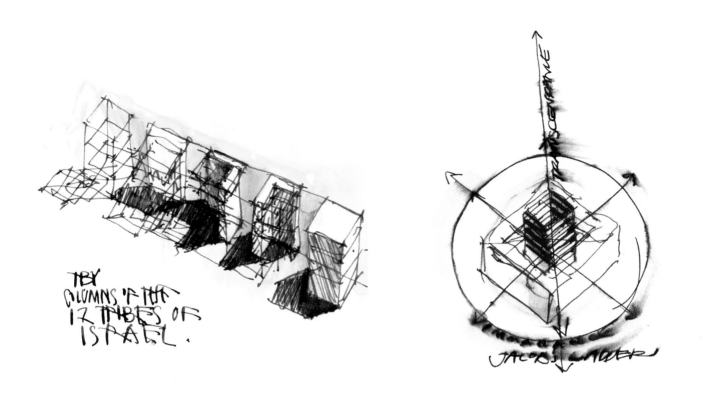

TRY
COLUMNS OF THE
12 TRIBES OF
ISRAEL.

JACOBS LADDER

Sketches

Sketches

Sketches

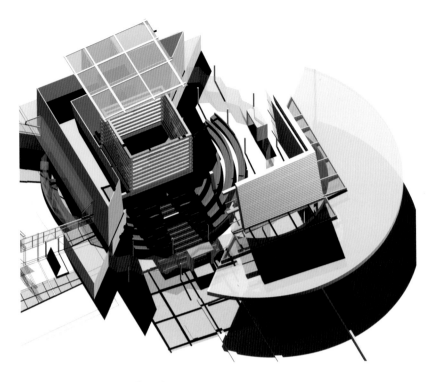

Axonometric view broken down into quarters

Isometric composition

Axonometry of the whole complex

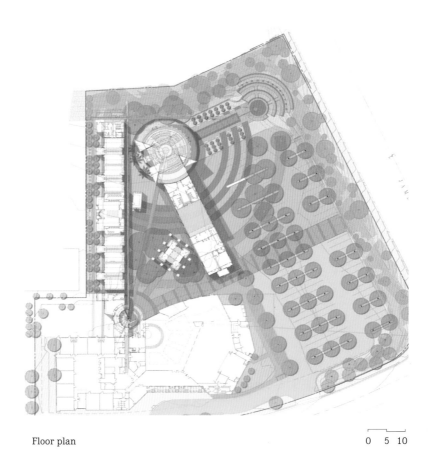

Floor plan

0 5 10

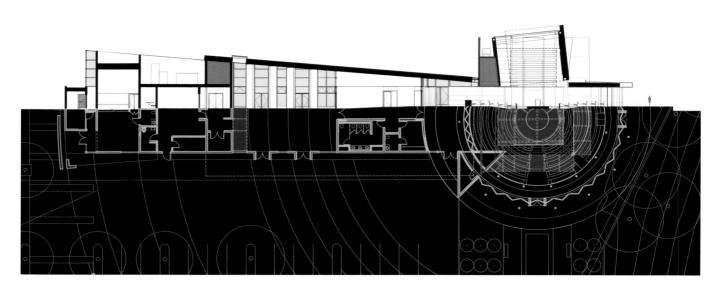

Section

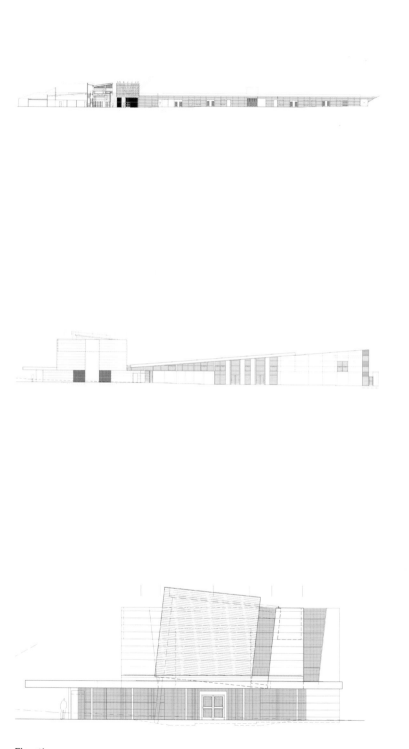

Elevations

Michael B. Lehrer founded Lehrer Architects in his native district of Los Feliz, Los Angeles, in 1985. The staff has extensive experience in community design and project management in the City of Angels. The studio has carried out numerous projects involving urban, residential, commercial and institutional works around the country, while keeping its roots in LA. The company's philosophy consists of top-quality architecture with a reflexive design that can produce happy and productive environments, as well as elegant, modern buildings.

## Lehrer Architects

# Abeijón Fernández

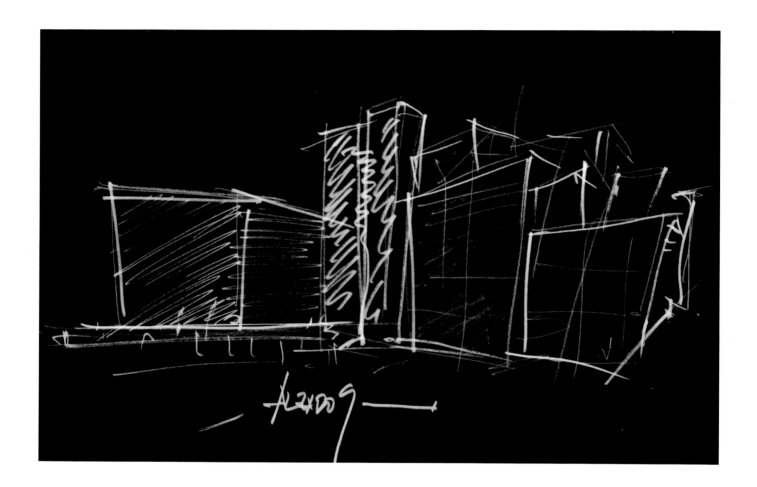

## Social and Cultural Center Castro de Riberas de Lea, Spain

■ This project is part of a municipal commission to create public spaces. The building, which the public had been requesting, was designed to satisfy the needs of young people and the elderly. The particular administrative organization of Galicia permits many small towns to enjoy this type of new facility. The architects took into account the use of the building – a space at the service of the community – and designed a multi-purpose, functional and dynamic place that would permit various activities. The three-storey building combines materials that create interesting textural contrasts – metal, glass and stone covering – and give it personality, offering an image in line with its public use.

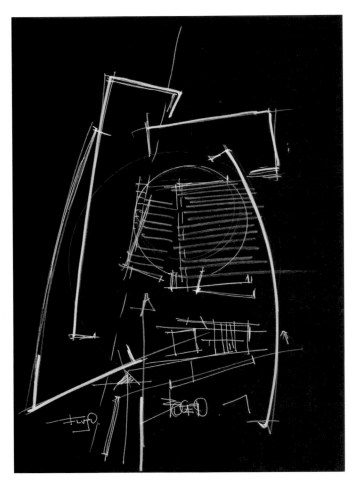

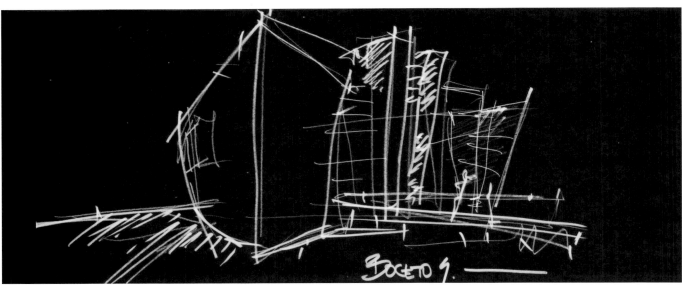

Sketches

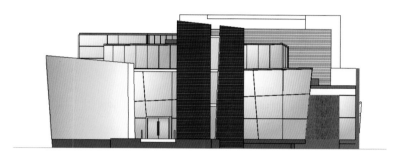

Front elevation

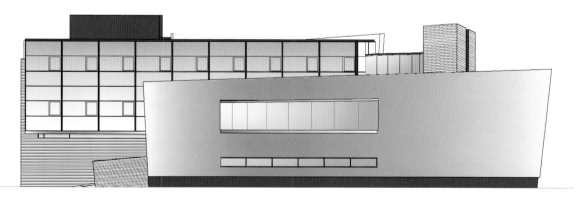

Side elevation

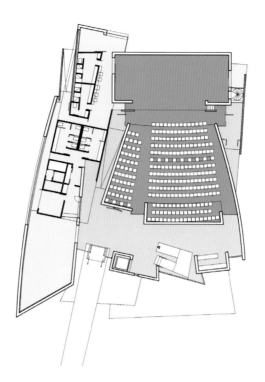

First floor

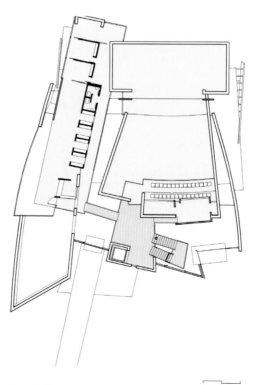

Second floor

0  2  4

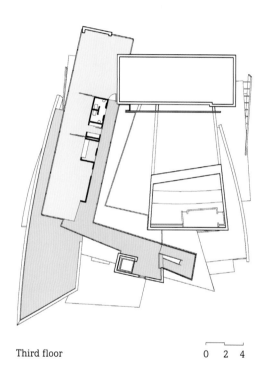

Third floor

0  2  4

José Abeijón Vela and Miguel Fernández Carreiras graduated from La Corunna School of Architecture to form a company in 1996. Since then they have designed and built numerous projects, including social-welfare buildings such as daycare centers, old people's homes and cultural and administrative buildings, as well as numerous residential complexes. The architects seek to establish a visual and formal complicity between work, site and the individual. On the basis of this premise they look for clarity and functional honesty, a rational distribution of space and the achievement of free and open areas.

## Abeijón Fernández

# Gatermann + Schossig

## Roman Museum Xanten Xanten, Germany

■ The location of the Xanten regional museum is considered an important Roman settlement north of the Alps. The new building has been erected in this historical context, i.e., on the foundations of a number of ancient thermal baths. The building limits are the same as those of the old defensive structure, so it is possible to appreciate the size of the thermal complex. The main structure is formed by steel frames positioned along the width of the old wall. The external cladding is a light membrane of glass and panels that gives the illusion the building is opening up upon entry. The exhibition floors are a continual surface inside the space. The forms emphasize the length of the hall and make it possible to appreciate its size.

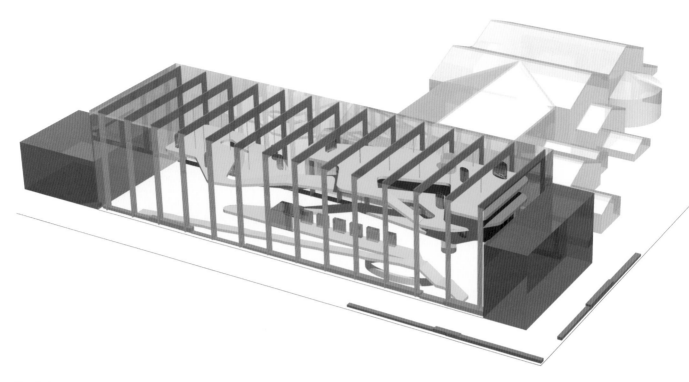

Renderings

Location Map

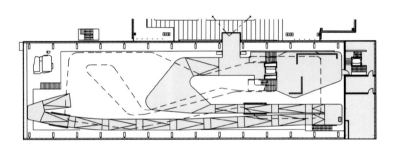

Level 0

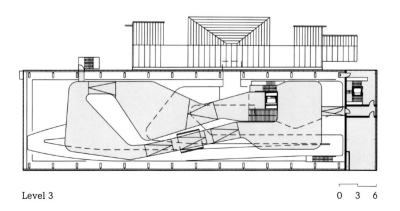

Level 3

0 3 6

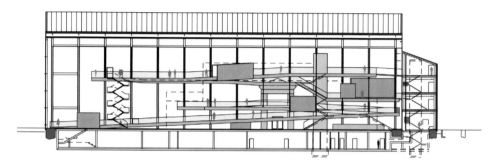

Longitudinal section of the museum

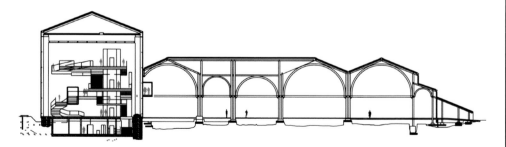

Transversal sections of the museum and the existing thermal defensive structure

The Gatermann + Schossig studio was founded in Cologne in 1984 by university professor Dörte Gatermann and Elmar Schossig. Its projects and implementations cover a wide variety of architectural disciplines, although work focuses particularly on buildings for industrial and administrative use. The architects' active participation in tenders has led them to win a great many awards and bids, as well as different architecture prizes for finished projects.

## Gatermann & Schossig

# Miguel Ángel Roca

# School of Medicine Córdoba, Argentina

■ This building faces north with one axis running parallel to the square, generating a north/south access. The first floor opens onto an interior courtyard which joins the building with the postgraduate school of business and other campus properties. From the outside it looks like a compact block of concrete, establishing a direct relationship with the rest of the campus. Upstairs, three common rooms open onto a central space that runs the length of the building. It is filled with light thanks to the side lights of variable width that illuminate the building interior. Natural light bathes the interiors of red-colored wood and generates a perfect atmosphere for a space designed to hold meetings.

© Miguel Ángel Roca

Sketches

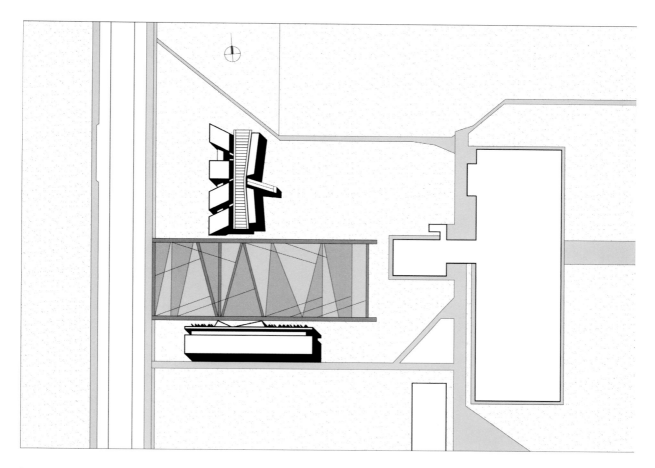

Location map

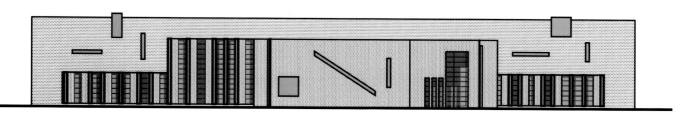

Elevation

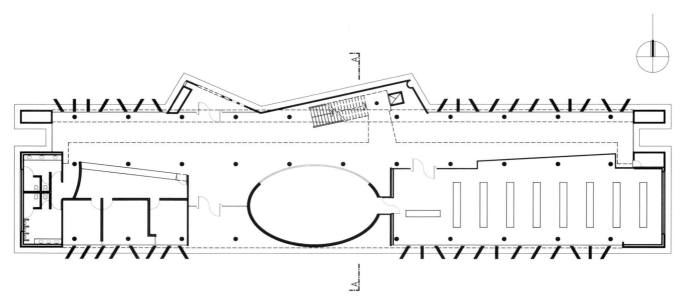

First floor

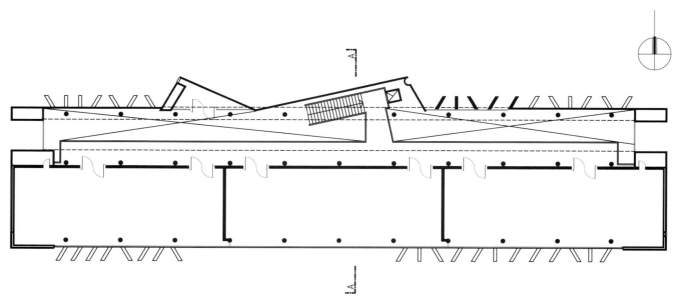

Second floor

0  2  4

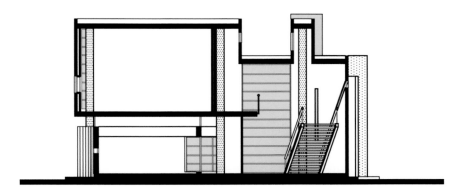

Section

■ Since graduating from the National University of Cordoba in 1965, Miguel Ángel Roca has built or begun the construction of more than 60 designs, including residential buildings, hospitals, civic and cultural centers, banks, offices, churches and squares, and has carried out numerous urban designs. He has worked as a professor in various universities across Latin America and been a guest lecturer in diverse centers of education around the world, such as the Paris-La Villette National School of Architecture and Rice University in Houston. He is also the author of numerous articles and his works have been included in different publications.

## Miguel Ángel Roca

41

# EMBT – Enric Miralles, Benedetta Tagliabue

## Santa Caterina Market Barcelona, Spain

■ The restoration of Santa Caterina Market involved locating the site in an ageless position in a point of time removed from both the ancient and new. The original building was not fully demolished and EMBT's work involved adding to existing elements. The method the studio follows is to reuse architecture, seeking a way to emphasize the best quality of each project. For this job, it proposed a design that would adapt to the complexity of the city and deliver on the public commitments undertaken. The best-known feature of the market, an entry point to the Santa Caterina neighborhood, is its brightly colored tiled roof. The architects also achieved a more rational organization of the accesses and fewer points of sale.

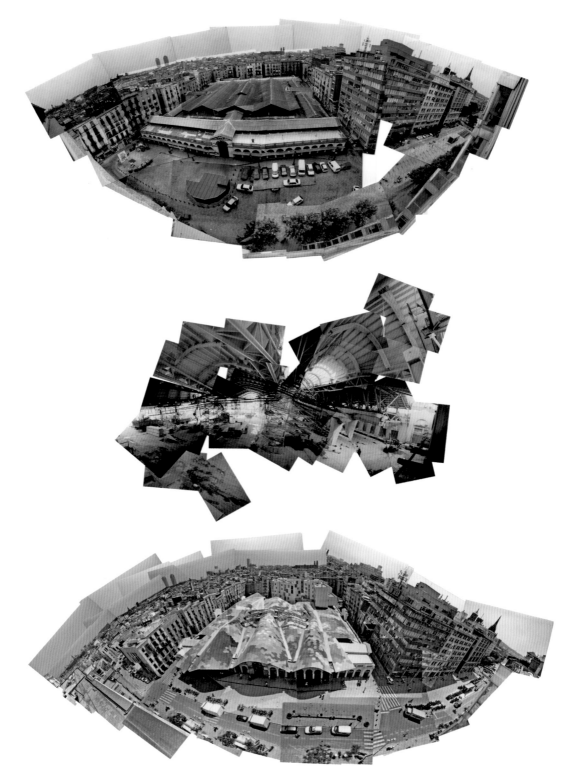

Photo montages

Photo montage

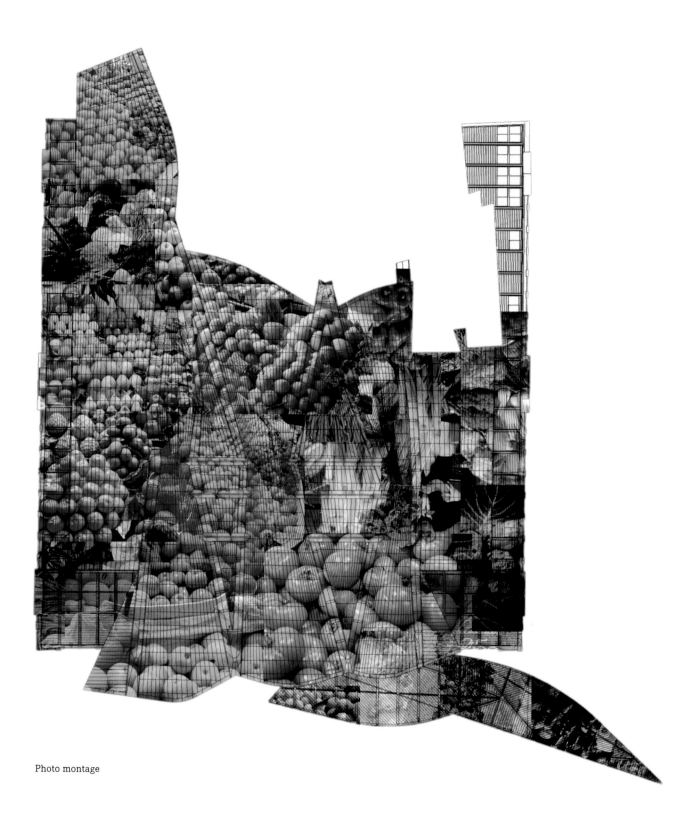

Photo montage

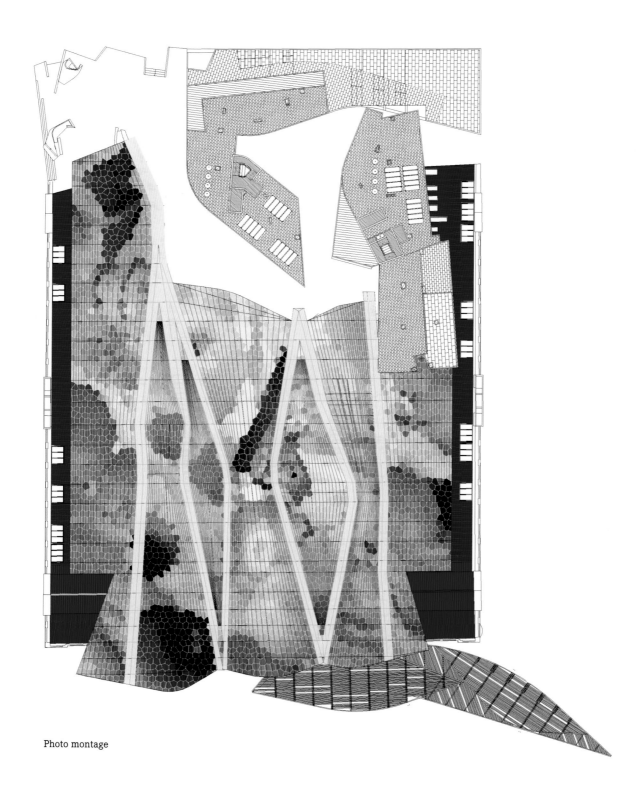

Photo montage

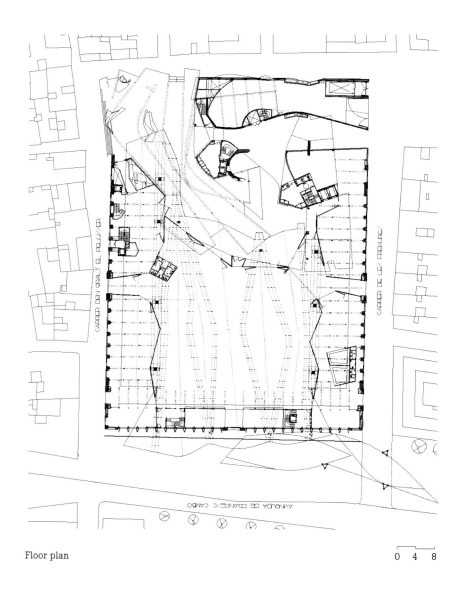

Floor plan

0 4 8

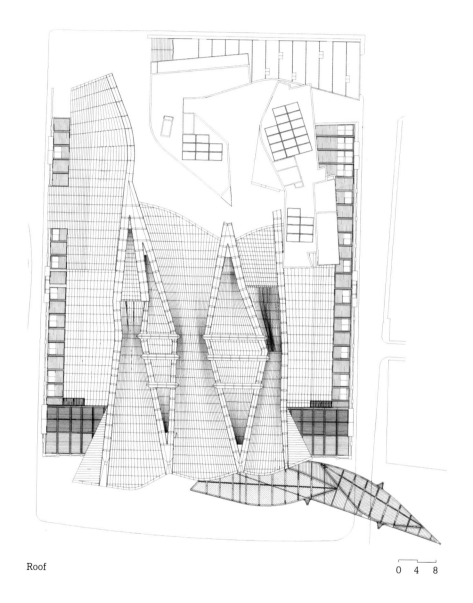

Roof

0 4 8

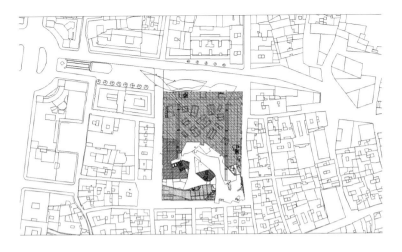

Location map

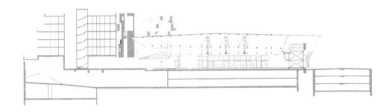

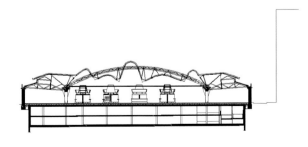

Sections

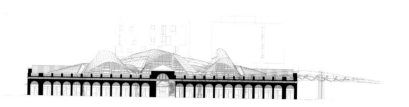

Elevations

EMBT Arquitectes Associats was founded in Barcelona in 1990 by Enric Miralles. Benedetta Tagliabue joined the studio in 1991 and it was renamed EMBT Arquitectes Associats. The main fields it works in are architecture, outdoor areas, town planning and exhibition centers. Its goal is to keep the spirit of Spanish and Italian architectural workshops alive, with a philosophy that involves paying particular attention to context. EMBT's works include a large number of major projects such as the roofs of Avenida Icaria in Barcelona for the 1992 Olympic Games, the Diagonal Mar park, the Hamburg School of Music and the Utrecht City Council building.

# EMBT – Enric Miralles, Benedetta Tagliabue

# Lehrer Architects, Gangi Design, Build (collaborators)

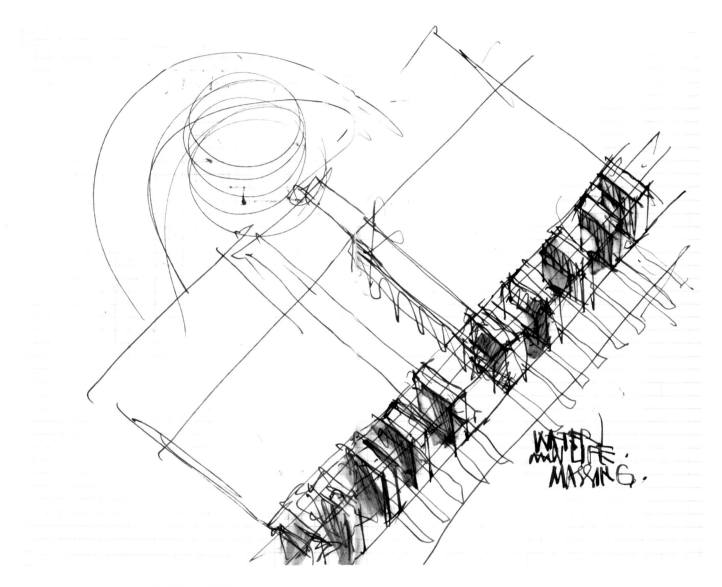

# Water and Life Museums Hemet, CA, USA

■ During the construction of the Diamond Valley Lake Reservoir, completed in 1998, a number of significant fossils were discovered that required an exhibition space. New buildings were then designed that would be connected by a large open terrace: the Water and Life Museums. Architecture and landscape were joined from the start of the project to function as a single entity. The buildings, of a fresh and modern design, generate a strong contrast with the arid landscape. The exterior and interior spaces are mixed with a structure formed of ventilated floors and glass walls. It is important to mention the project's sustainability and ecology, which has seen it pick up various specialist awards. It is also the first museum building to secure a Platinum LEED (Leadership in Energy and Environmental Design) rating.

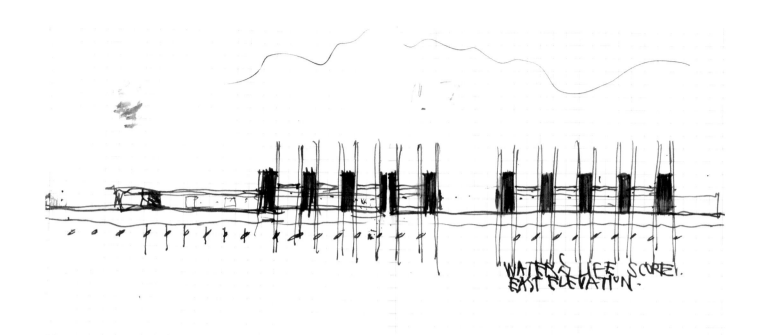

WATER & LIFE SCORE.
EAST ELEVATION.

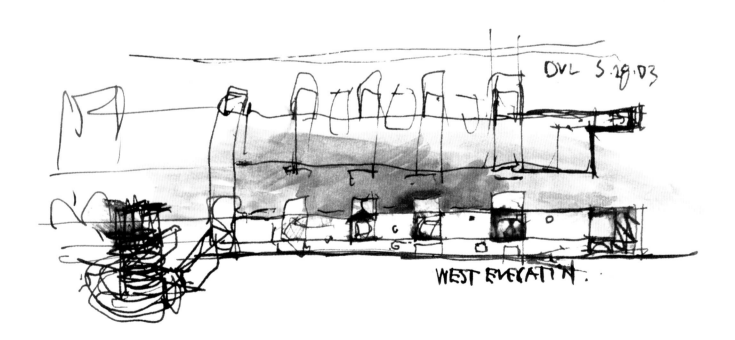

DVL 5.29.03

WEST ELEVATION.

Sketches

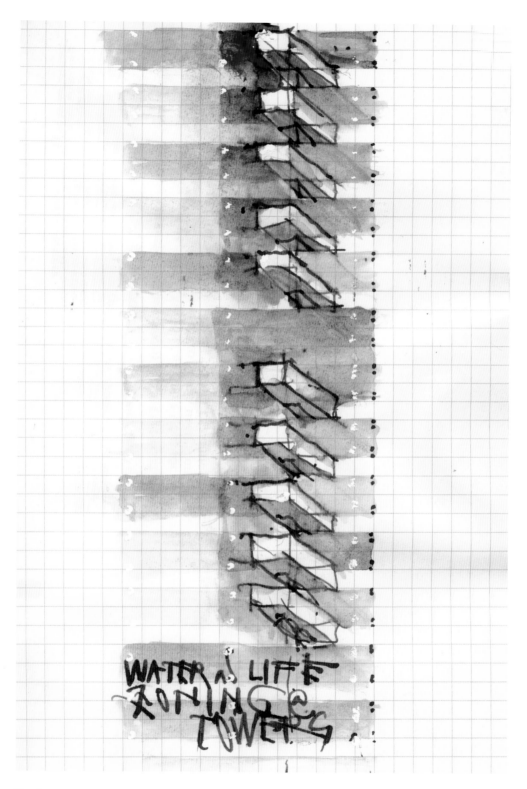

Sketch

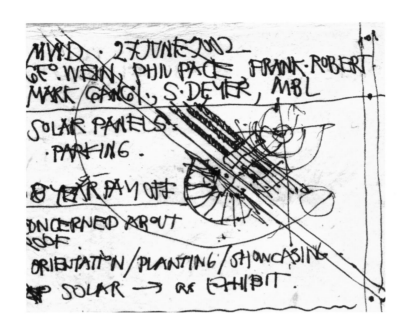

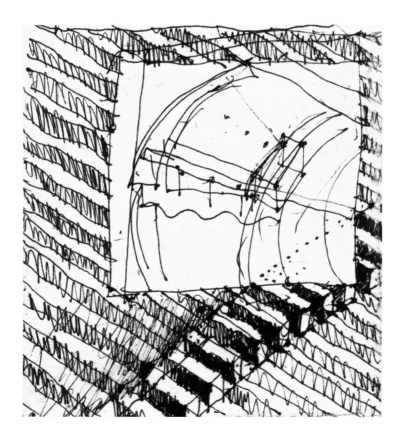

Sketches

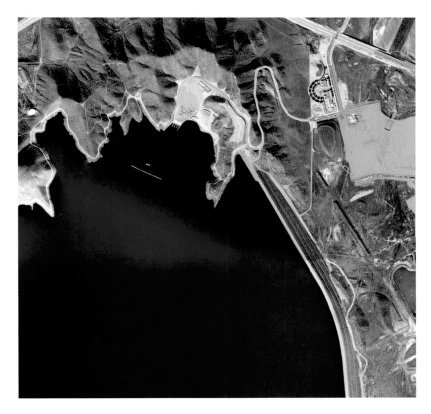

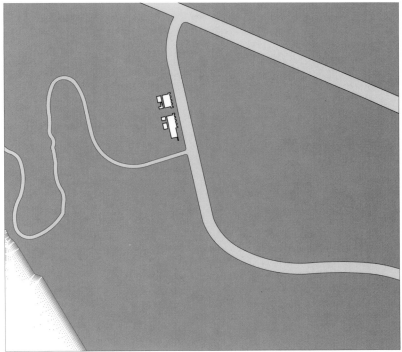

Location maps

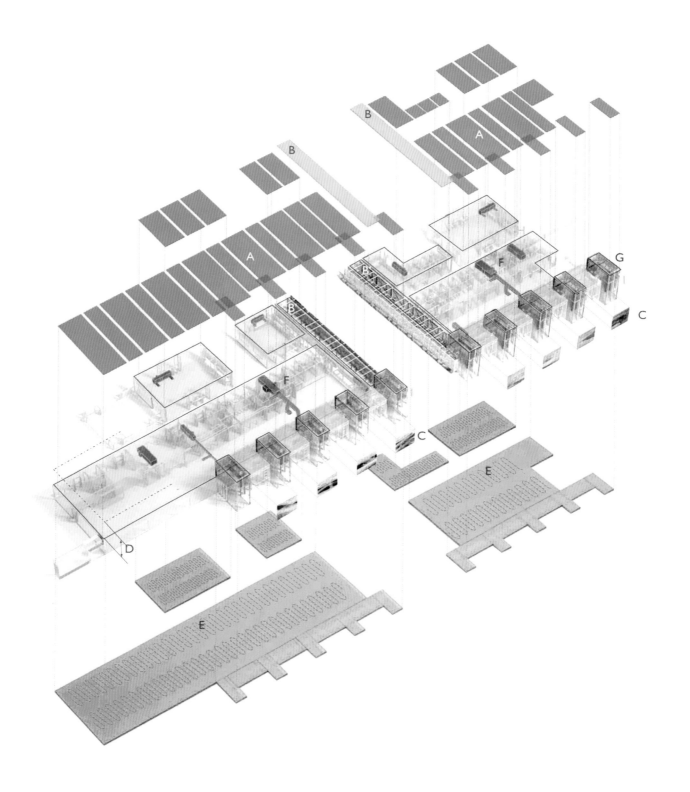

Diagram of the sustainable elements

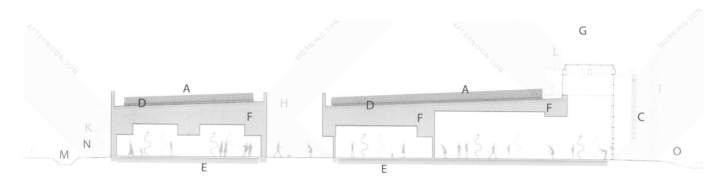

Section. Diagram of the sustainable elements

Building rendering

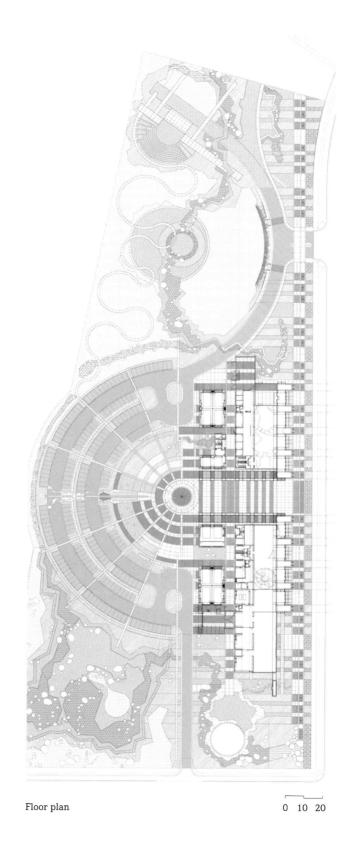

Floor plan

0  10  20

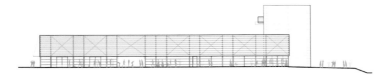

Elevations

Section

■ Michael B. Lehrer founded Lehrer Architects in his native district of Los Feliz, Los Angeles, in 1985. The staff has extensive experience in community design and project management in the City of Angels. The studio has carried out numerous projects involving urban, residential, commercial and institutional works around the country, while keeping its roots in LA. The company's philosophy consists of top-quality architecture with a reflexive design that can produce happy and productive environments, as well as elegant, modern buildings.

**Lehrer Architects**

# EMBT – Enric Miralles, Benedetta Tagliabue

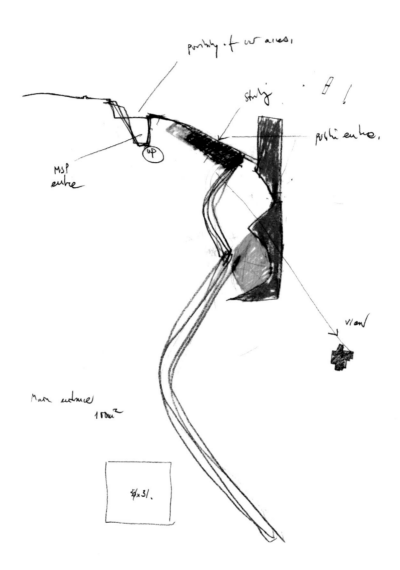

# Scottish Parliament Building Edinburgh, United Kingdom

■ The concept of the Scottish Parliament building was based on one main idea: it had to be capable of reflecting the land it represents. From the start the studio worked with the idea of individual identification with the land leading to collective awareness. Another concept included was the belief that land is a material that forms an indispensable part of a project. The architects bore in mind that, although located in Edinburgh, the Parliament pertains to all the Scots and the Scottish land. This intense relationship between land, people and architecture is evidenced in a small-scale building but one designed to be seen from afar, like John Knox's Royal Mile. A psychological approach to architecture replaces the idea of a monumental building.

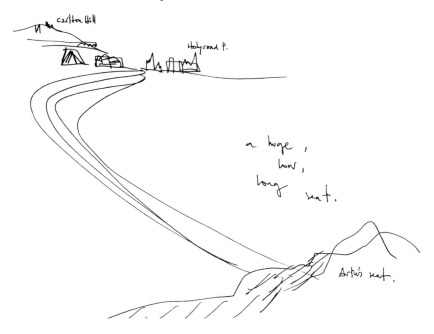

A story definition is needed.

Calton Hill

Holyrood P.

a huge,
low,
long seat.

Arthu's seat.

Sketch

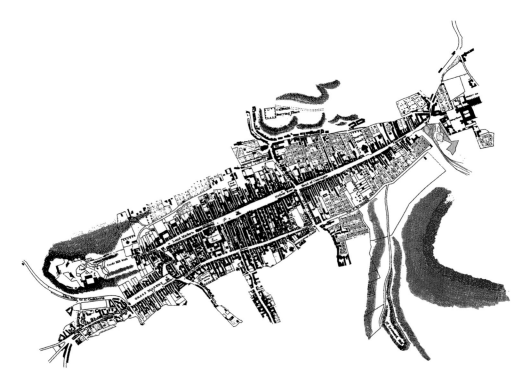

Location map

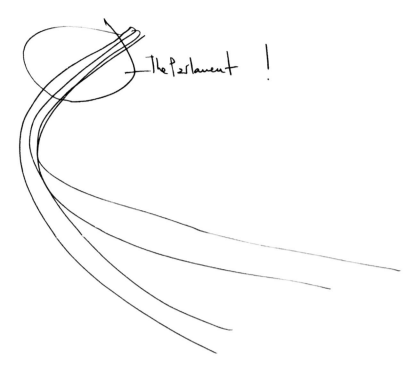

Sketch

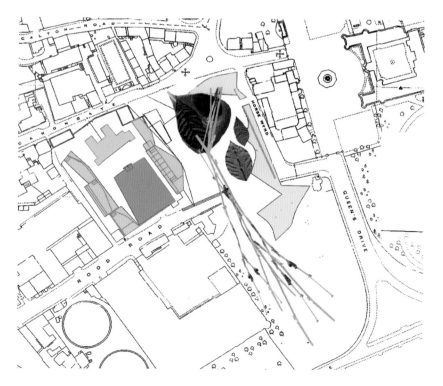

Location map

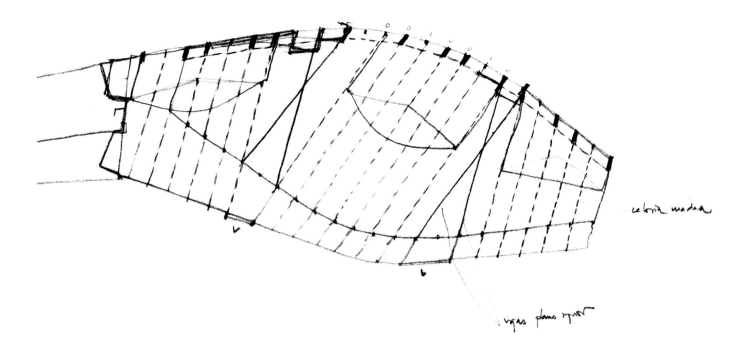

Sketches

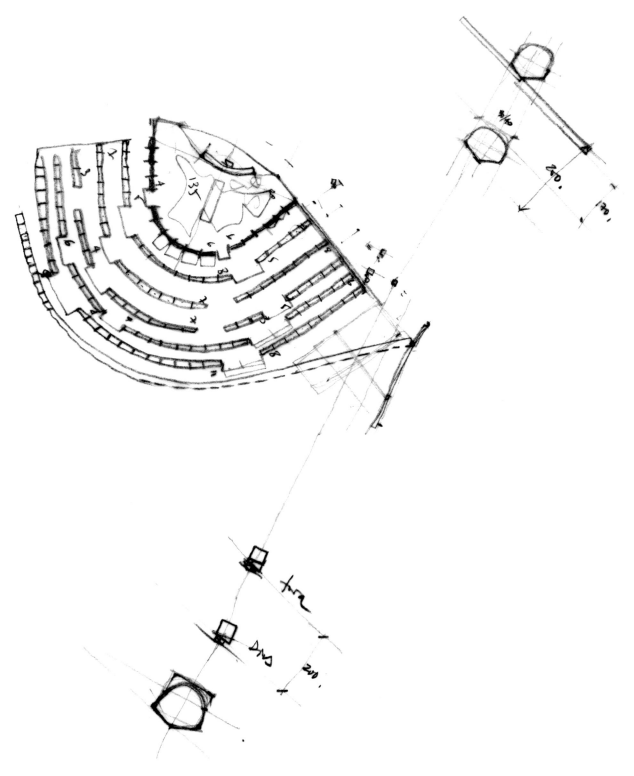

Sketch

Garden level

0  5  10

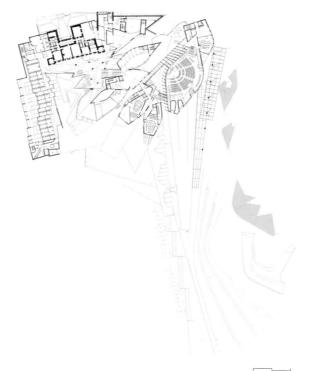

First level

0  10  20

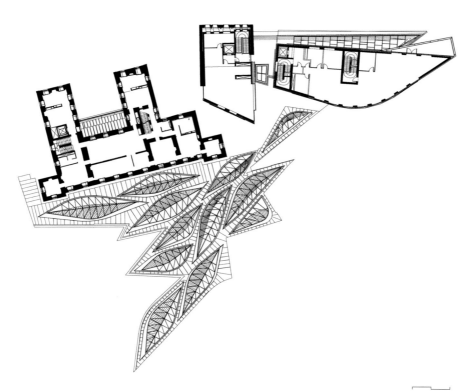

Second level

0  3  6

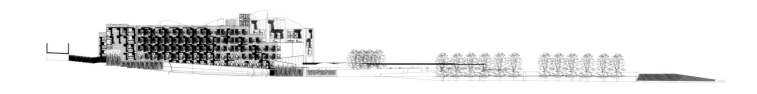

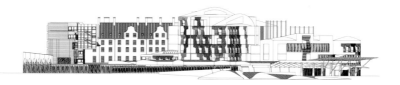

Elevations

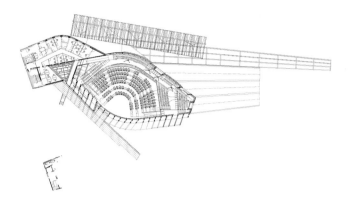

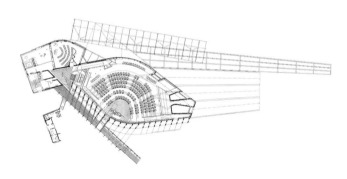

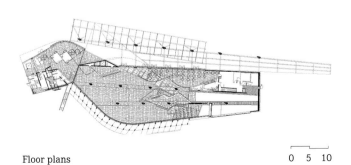

Floor plans

0   5   10

■ EMBT Arquitectes Associats was founded in Barcelona in 1990 by Enric Miralles. Benedetta Tagliabue joined the studio in 1991 and it was renamed EMBT Arquitectes Associats. The main fields it works in are architecture, outdoor areas, town planning and exhibition centers. Its goal is to keep the spirit of Spanish and Italian architectural workshops alive, with a philosophy that involves paying particular attention to context. EMBT's works include a large number of major projects such as the roofs of Avenida Icaria in Barcelona for the 1992 Olympic Games, the Diagonal Mar park, the Hamburg School of Music and the Utrecht City Council building.

## EMBT – Enric Miralles, Benedetta Tagliabue

# Satoshi Okada Architects

# Agri-Community Center Taisanji district, prefecture of Shiga, Japan

■ This building is a public facility for the farming community in the Taisanji district. For years, especially during World War II, agriculture was protected by the Japanese government, but the transformation of the industrial structure and the reestablishment of agricultural imports led to an important fall in the sector. The goal of this building is to revitalize the community, promoting exchanges between farmers and city dwellers. The multi-purpose building can house agricultural presentations or culinary events featuring local produce. The Agri-Community Center has been built with a wooden structure to which CCS, a system of elements that work like structures developed by Satoshi Okada and Hirokazu Toki, is then applied.

73

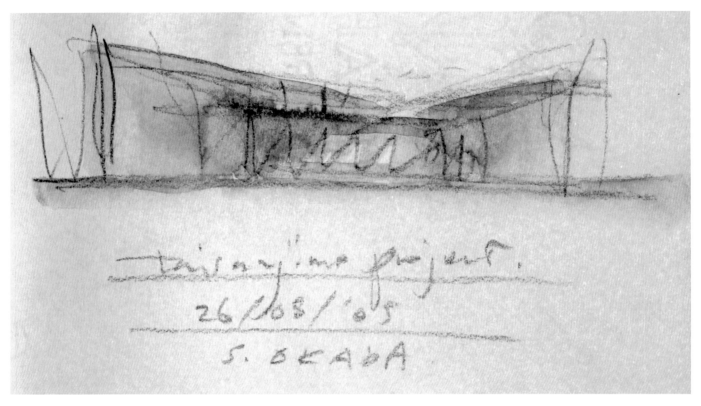

Sketches

Sketch

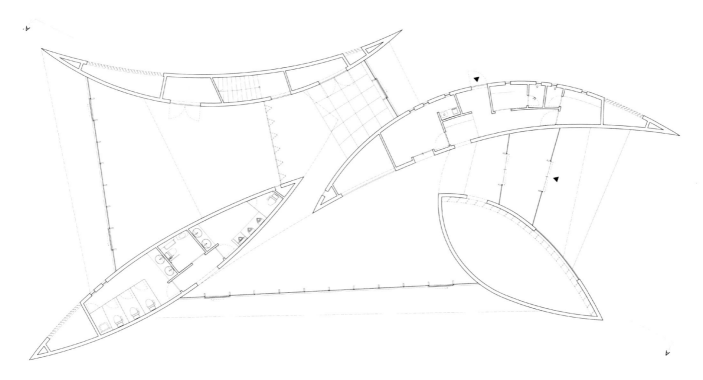

First floor

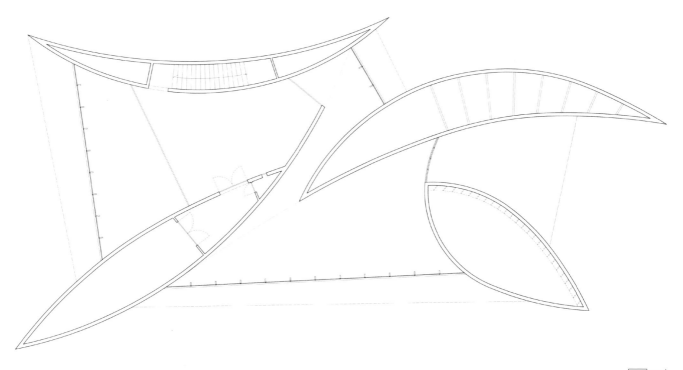

Second floor

0  1  2

Section

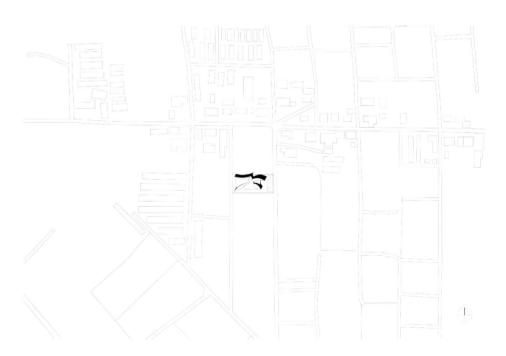

Location map

■ Satoshi Okada graduated from the Architecture School of Columbia University, New York, in 1989. He studied there until 1997 under Kenneth Frampton. International recognition arrived in the year 2000 with the Mount Fuji project, the subject of extensive study. His works range from residential projects to public buildings. He is currently working in his architectural practice and teaching at the School of Environmental Design, where he has founded the Institute for Design and the Environment (IDEA). He is frequently invited to lecture in universities around the world.

## Satoshi Okada
## Architects

# Patel Taylor

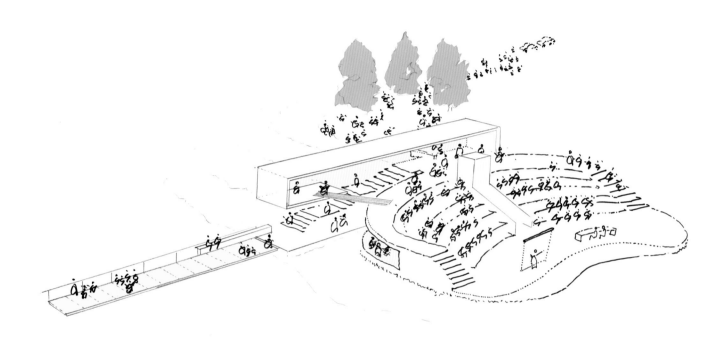

## Wivenhoe Lecture Hall Colchester, United Kingdom

■ Wivenhoe Lecture Hall is located in the middle of the Essex University campus. Its construction involved the creation of a new symbol for the university. The main function of the auditorium is to provide a 1,000-seat space for conferences and other academic activities. A flexible design means it can be divided into two independent lecture halls, adding value to the project. The building, semi-interred on a sloping plot of land, connects with the main campus via an axial route, and a staircase frames the view of a nearby lake. The lozenge-shaped structure is made from concrete. The roof is held up by a combination of laminated wood and steel beams. Outside, of note is the stainless steel cladding and a glass projection housing the reception area.

© Charlotte Wood

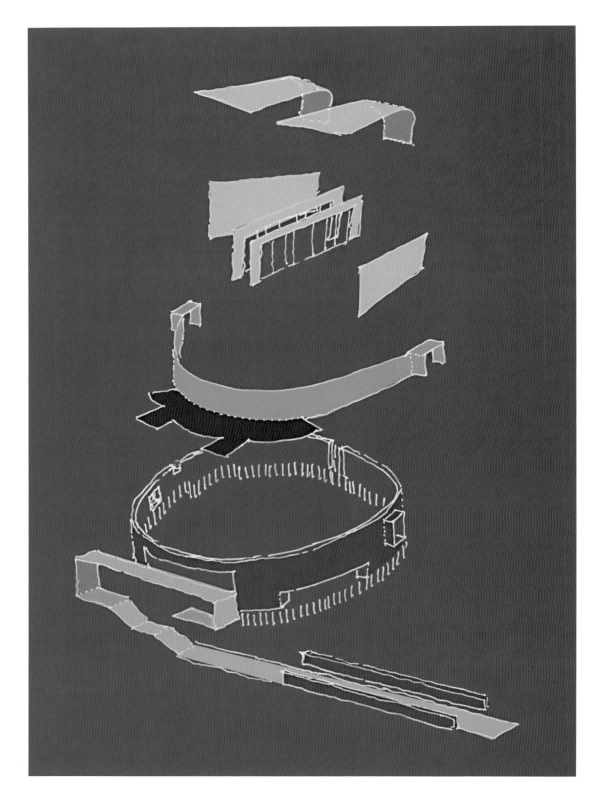

Exploded view

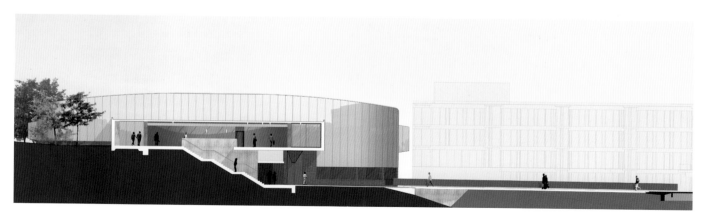

Renderings

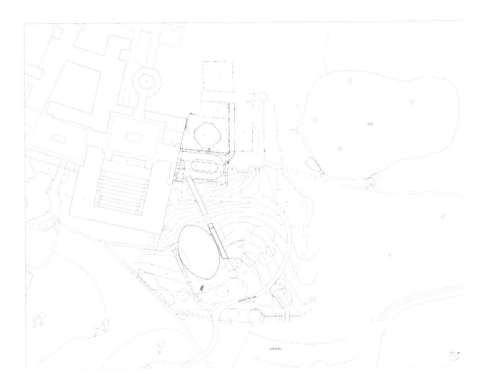

Location map

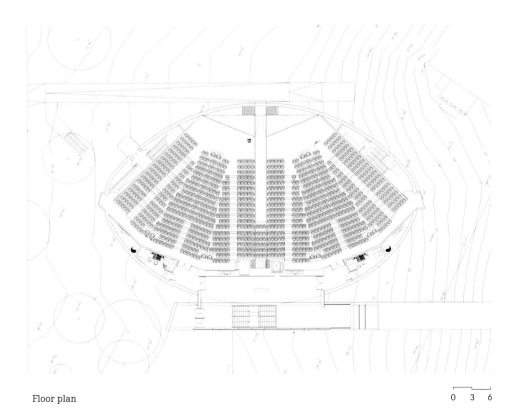

Floor plan

0  3  6

Sections

**Patel Taylor**

# Steven Holl Architects

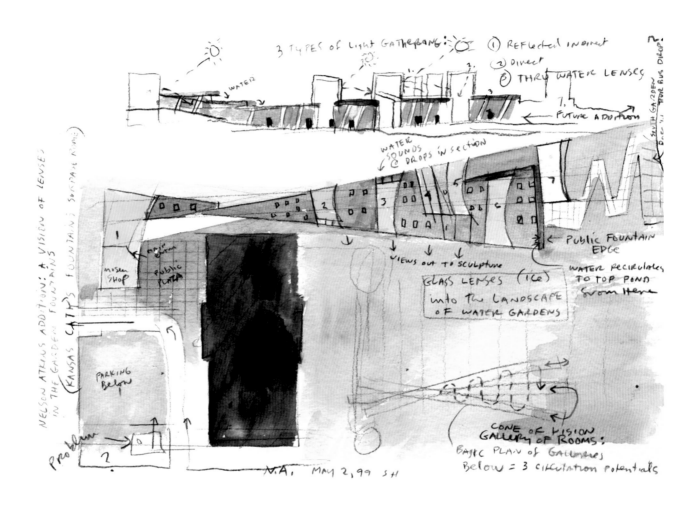

# Expansion of the Nelson-Atkins Museum Kansas City, MO, USA

■ The expansion of the Nelson-Atkins Museum of Art merges architecture and landscape in an experimental design to be perceived individually by each visitor. A sculpture park and the new expansion, called the Bloch Building, have transformed the site into a unique space. The Bloch Building runs the eastern limit of the campus and is distinguished by five glass 'lenses' between the existing 1933 building and the sculpture park. This creates a place with new spaces and angles of vision. The 'lenses' are transparent buildings illuminated by sunlight during the day and which at night shine in the background thanks to the light they transmit. The five shapes combine transparency, opacity, tranquility and peace.

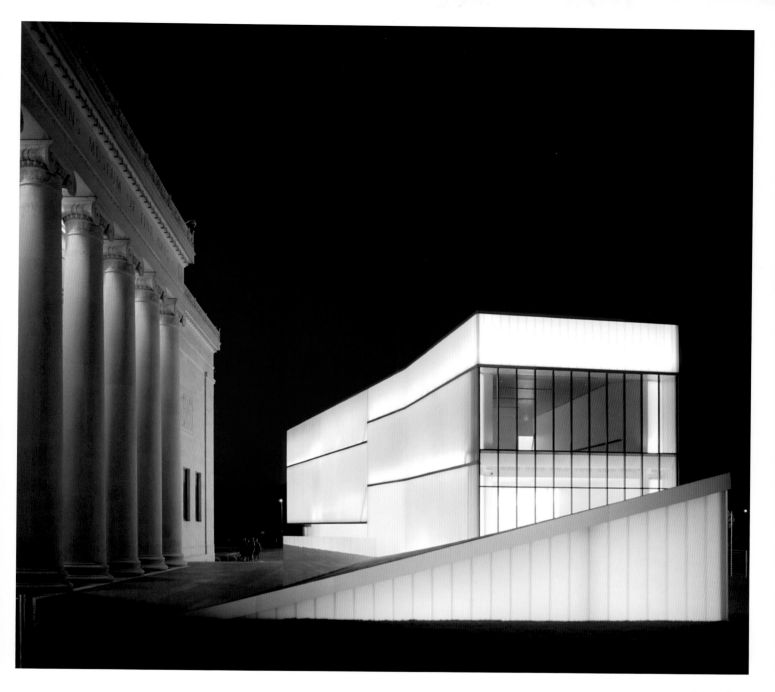

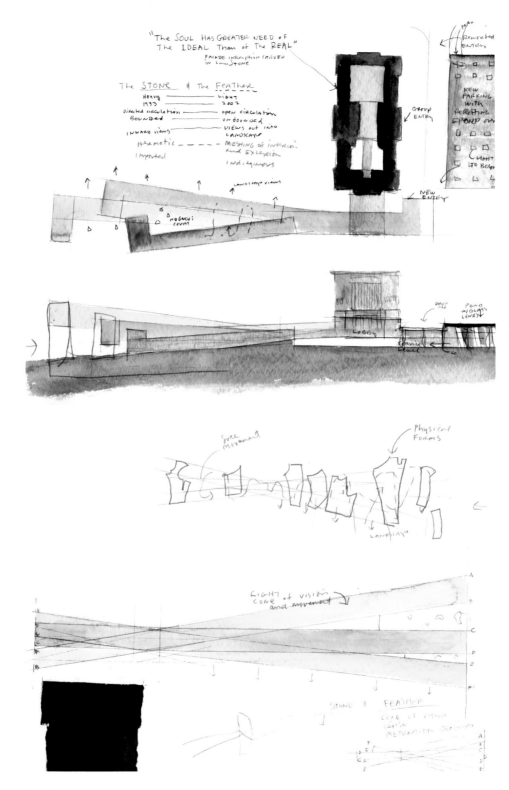

"The SOUL HAS GREATER NEED of
THE IDEAL Than of The REAL"
FACADE inscription CARVED
in limeStone

THE STONE & THE FEATHER
HEAVY ——————— LIGHT
1933 ——————— 2002
directed circulation ——— open circulation
BOUNDED ——————— unbounded
INWARD views ——————— VIEWS out into
                        LANDSCAPE
HERMETIC ─ ─ ─ ─ ── MESHING OF INTERIOR
                        and EXTERIOR
imported            indigenous

Sketches

86

Model

Rendering

Sketches

Renderings

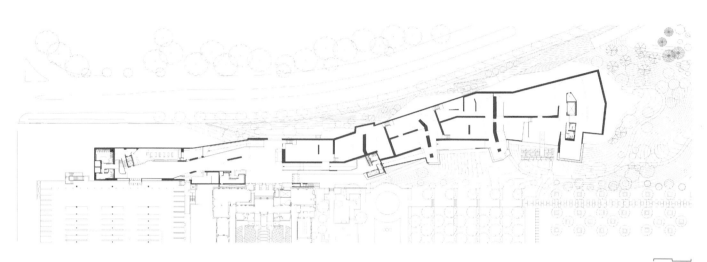

First floor

0 10 20

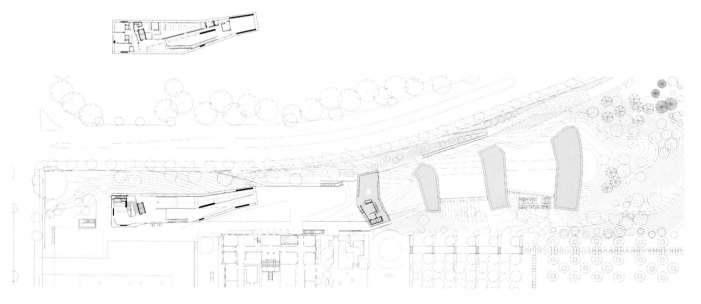

Second floor

0 8 16

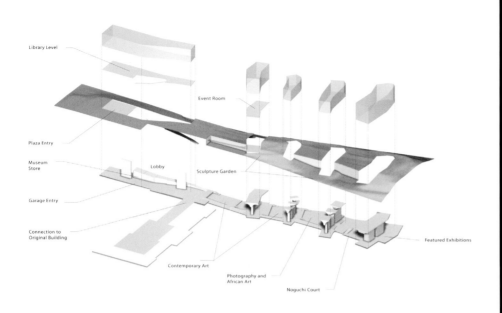

Library Level

Event Room

Plaza Entry

Museum
Store

Lobby

Sculpture Garden

Garage Entry

Connection to
Original Building

Featured Exhibitions

Contemporary Art

Photography and
African Art

Noguchi Court

Axonometric diagram

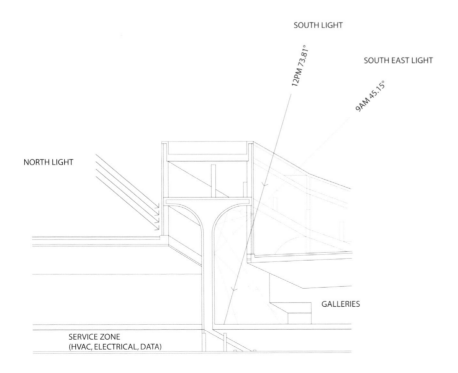

SOUTH LIGHT

12PM 73.81°

SOUTH EAST LIGHT

9AM 45.15°

NORTH LIGHT

GALLERIES

SERVICE ZONE
(HVAC, ELECTRICAL, DATA)

Diagram of the inside of the 'lenses'

■ Steven Holl was born in Bremerton, Washington in 1947. He graduated from the University of Washington and went on to study architecture in Rome in 1970. In 1976 he founded Steven Holl Architects in New York, a studio which today has offices in New York and Beijing and 49 people on staff. The company's work has been published and exhibited on many occasions and received numerous awards. He is considered one of America's premier architects and his work is recognized for its ability to combine space and light with a great sensitivity for context.

**Steven Holl
Architects**

# RMJM HK

# University of Shenzen Library Shenzen, China

■ The new library at the University of Shenzen, finished in 2007, is a fresh icon for local facilities, the entry to a campus which also includes faculties of the University of Beijing and Nakai University. The design had to include the concepts of modernity and unity, so the architects decided on a large and undulating volume like the hills that surround the campus. Contemporary materials aim to reflect the erudite language of knowledge. One of the most important features of the building is the pedestrian bridge that crosses the Dasha River and joins the two zones of the urban plan. The library, which also acts as the local public library, is another element in the plan designed to provide much-needed infrastructures and services to one of the country's fastest-growing cities.

© H.G. Esch Photography

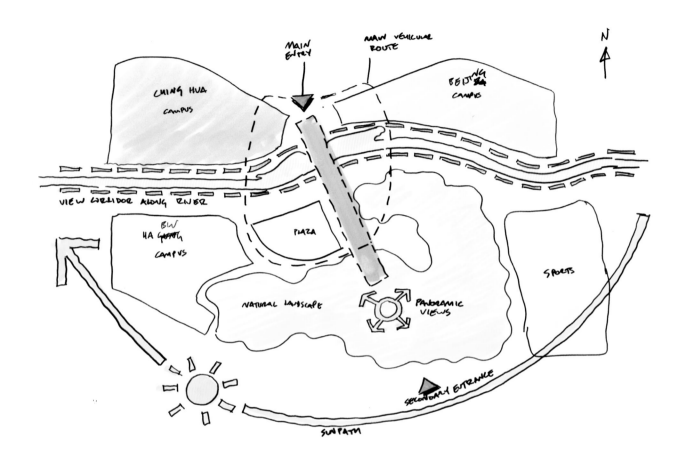

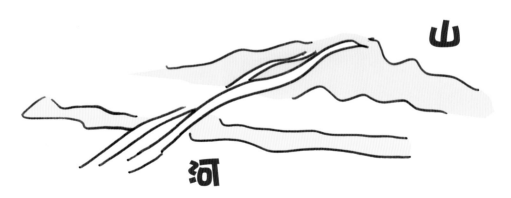

Sketches

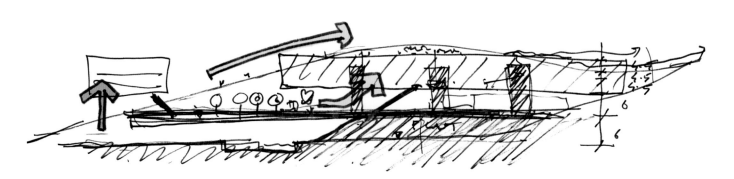

Sketches

Sketches

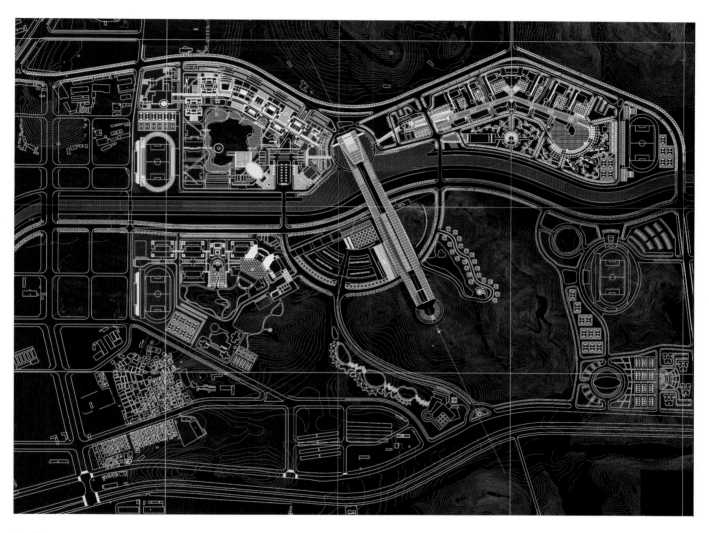

Location map

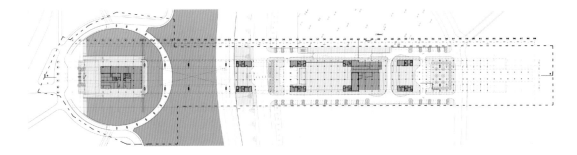

Level 1

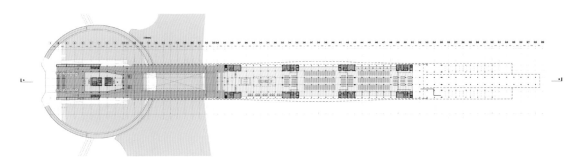

Level 2

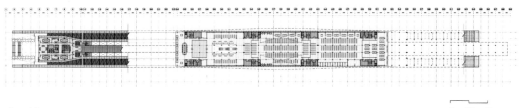

Level 3

0 20 40

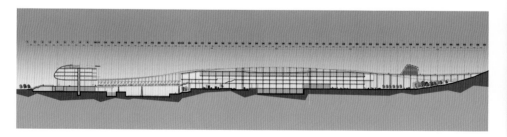

Level 4

0  20  40

Section

RMJM HK is an architectural studio based in the United Kingdom, with offices in Europe, Asia, the Middle East and North America. The 1,100-plus employees provide architecture, interior-design and town-planning services and work on the conservation of historical and landscape heritages and in computer design. RMJM HK is committed to top-quality design that connects places with people, context and culture to form modern and dynamic architecture. The project managers on this work were Scott Findley, Jiang Chun, William Wong, Robert MacKenzie and Edmond La.

## RMJM HK

# Miguel Ángel Roca

## Postgraduate School of Business Córdoba, Argentina

■ The building was designed in the shape of a north-south running column - in fact, a common area surrounded by wooden walls, opens up toward the sides and upward. One side has four large conference rooms, representing four rocks or stone blocks, separated by common areas such as the bar, maintenance rooms and storage spaces. The covering of these spaces, both with regards the walls and floor, is mostly cedar wood. Study rooms distributed on two levels are at the other end. The design of the outside is a robust volume that looks like stone. Around it is a landscaped square that communicates with other university buildings, such as the school of medicine and the management offices.

101

Sketch

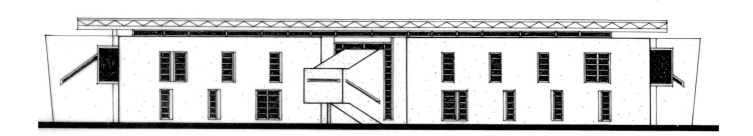

East elevation

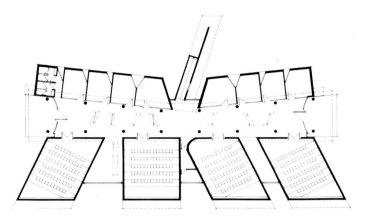

First floor

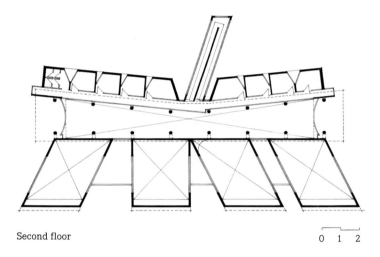

Second floor

0 1 2

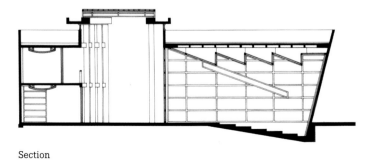

Section

■ Since graduating from the National University of Cordoba in 1965, Miguel Ángel Roca has built or begun the construction of more than 60 designs, including residential buildings, hospitals, civic and cultural centers, banks, offices, churches and squares, and has carried out numerous urban designs. He has worked as a professor in various universities across Latin America and been a guest lecturer in diverse centers of education around the world, such as the Paris-La Villette National School of Architecture and Rice University in Houston. He is also the author of numerous articles and his works have been included in different publications.

## Miguel Ángel Roca

# Arteks Arquitectura, Esther Pascal

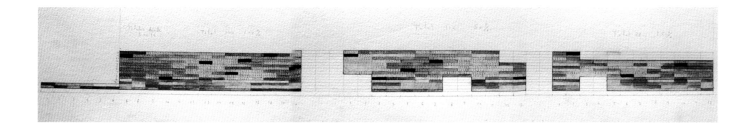

# Congress Center Ordino, Andorra

■ The Congress Center in Ordino is a large facility for this small region of just 4,000 inhabitants. The building has the capacity and facilities required to hold any type of event, from a congress or meeting through to exhibitions, shows, etc. It has been fitted with the latest technology and enjoys an excellent location- just 10 minutes from the capital city. The main foyer, located on the first floor, has spectacular views over Ordino Valley. There are also three modular rooms, one that can in turn be subdivided into two. The foyer stands out for its ceiling composed of sheets of wood and walls covered with the building materials also used on the façades.

© Pedro Pegenaute

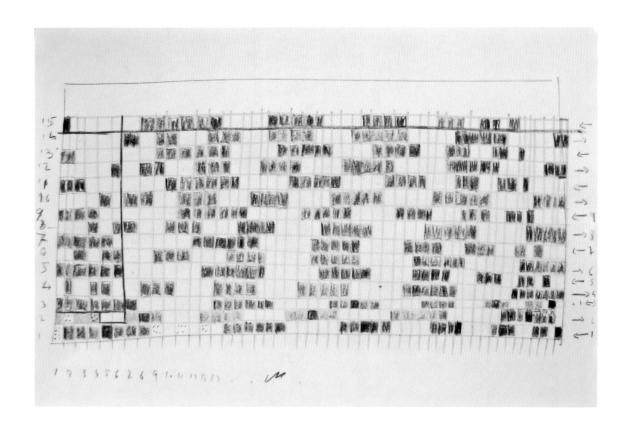

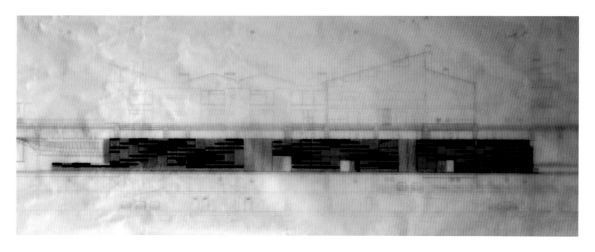

Sketches

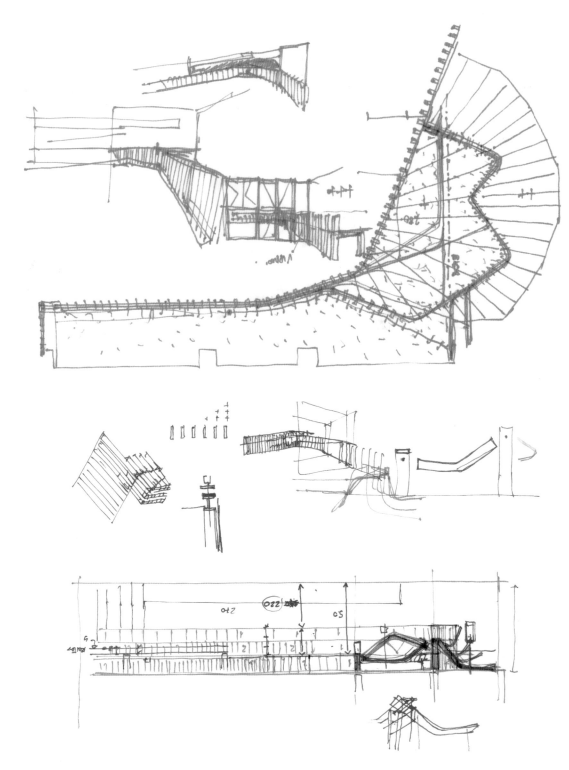

Sketches

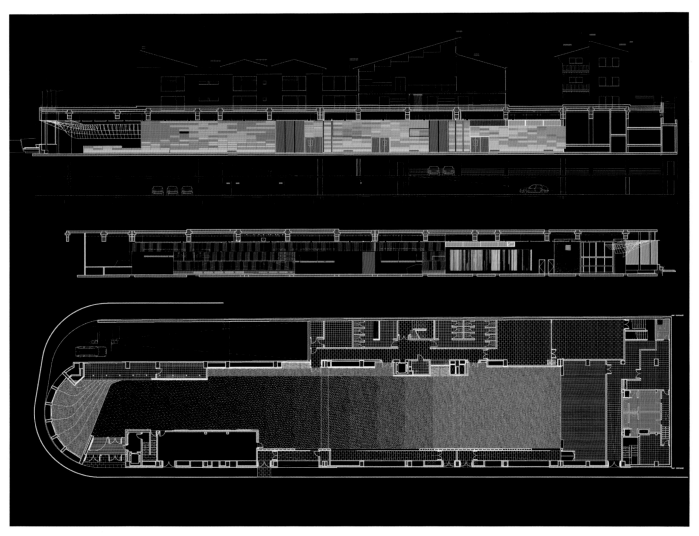

Elevation, section and floor plan

0  3  6

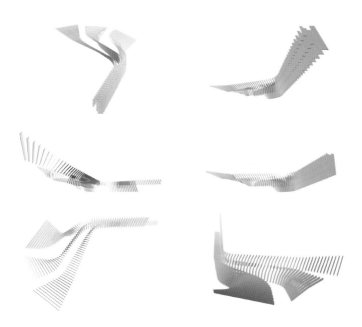

Detail of the sheets of wood on the ceiling

Renderings

■ Arteks Arquitectura was founded in 2002. Its architectural, design and town-planning projects are mainly carried out in Spain and Andorra. The founding partners are the architects Elisabet Faura and Gerard Veciana, designers of the Països Catalans Park in Vila Seca. For the Congress Center project they worked with Esther Pascal, an architect with a solid background in public works and winner of various competitions.

## Arteks Arquitectura, Esther Pascal

# Ona Arquitectes

## Port Rodó Infants and Primary School Camprodó, Spain

■ The new school building is located in an expanding area of a small town in Tarragona province. It runs perpendicular to the street, with numerous advantages: it established a visual relationship with the rural and urban environment and minimized the need to move earth during construction, which meant the old school building could be maintained while the new one was being built. The work involved an alternative to prefabricated buildings, i.e., it was built in changeable independent layers: a structural layer, a waterproofing layer, a thermal layer, the top layer, etc. This allowed speedy changes during any phase of the work at a very low cost. The result is a variable, flexible building.

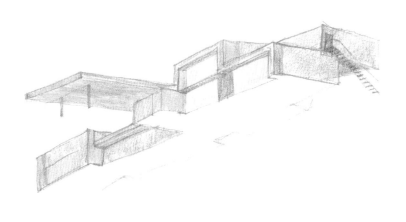

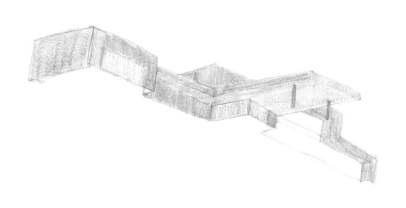

Sketches

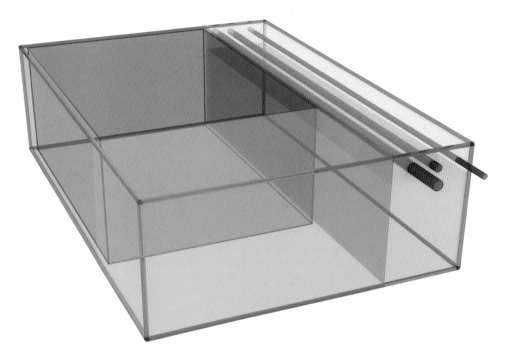

Module outline

Structural module

Library module

2 classrooms module and corridor

Classroom module, corridor and service area

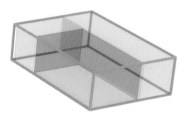

Classroom module, corridor-porch

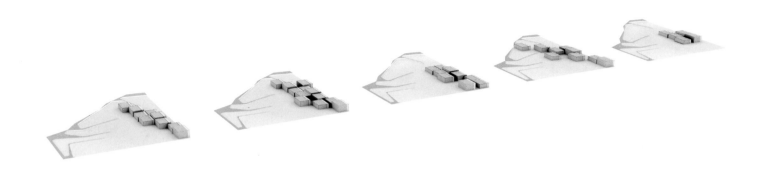

Outline of the different organization of module designs

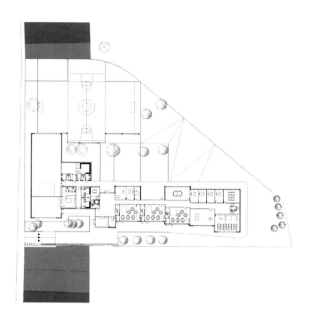

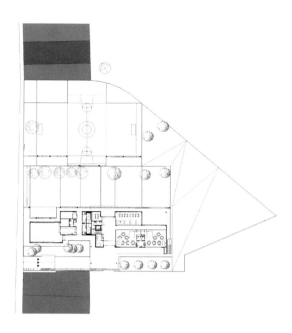

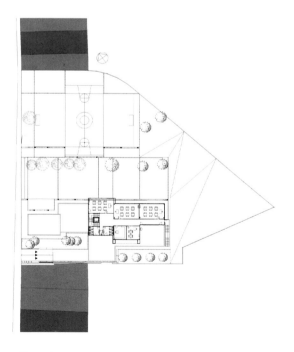

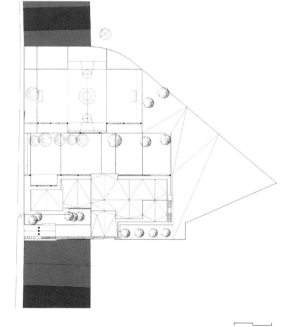

Floor plans

0   8   16

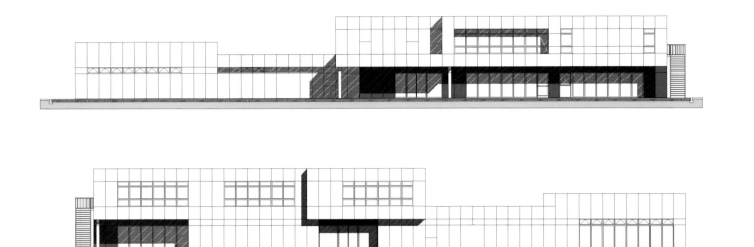

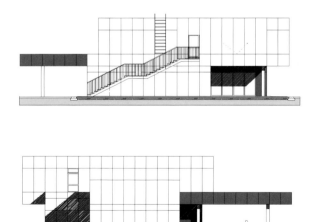

Elevations

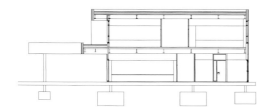

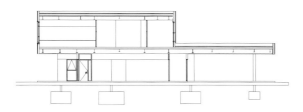

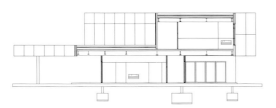

Cross sections

■ Ona Arquitectes is an architectural, urban-planning and design company created in Barcelona in 1997. Its founders are the architects Pedro Ondoño Solís and Silvia Font Llorensí. Throughout its history, Ona Arquitectes has worked on projects for a broad market, from private customers through to companies, investors and projects for the public administration. Ona Arquitectes has won numerous national and international tenders. It currently has offices in Cordoba (Spain) and Santiago (Chile). In May 2008 Ona Arquitectes merged with Espinet Ubach Arquitectes Associats to form the studio Euplus.

**Ona Arquitectes**

# G. Vázquez Consuegra

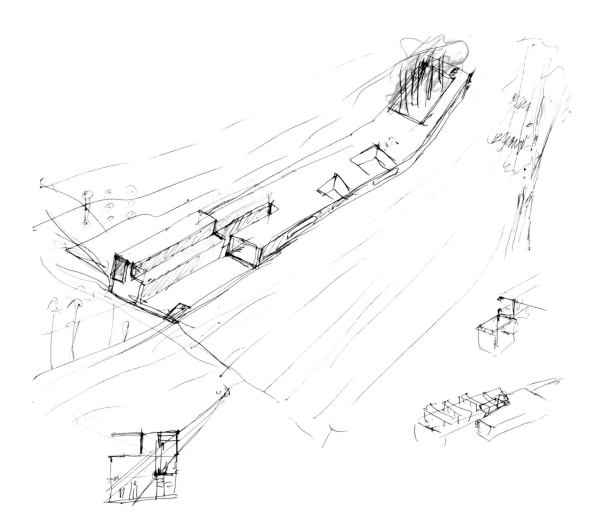

# Baelo Claudia Visitors Center Baelo Claudia archeological site, Spain

■ The building proposed by the architects is a low volume distributed over two levels, minimizing its visual impact on the magnificent landscape. The fact that the building lies on sharply sloping land made this location necessary, particularly in order to prevent it from overexposure to the dominant winds and to economize on resources. The construction consists of a single compact volume which is closed and dense and which opens only onto the four courtyards that provide natural lighting and ventilation, achieving a look of greater abstraction suitable for this small institutional building. The organization of spaces divides the design into two areas: public and internal, the latter being where the conservation, administration and research services are housed.

Sketches

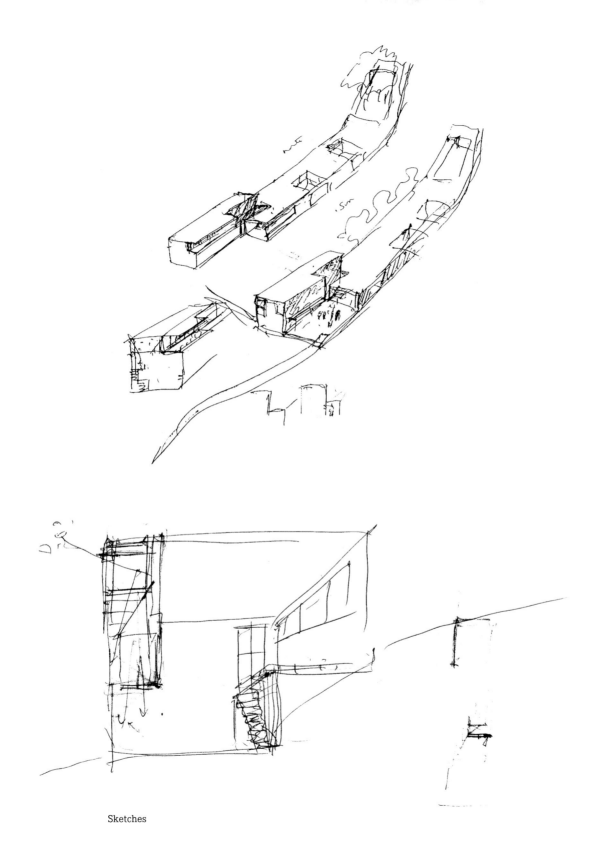

Sketches

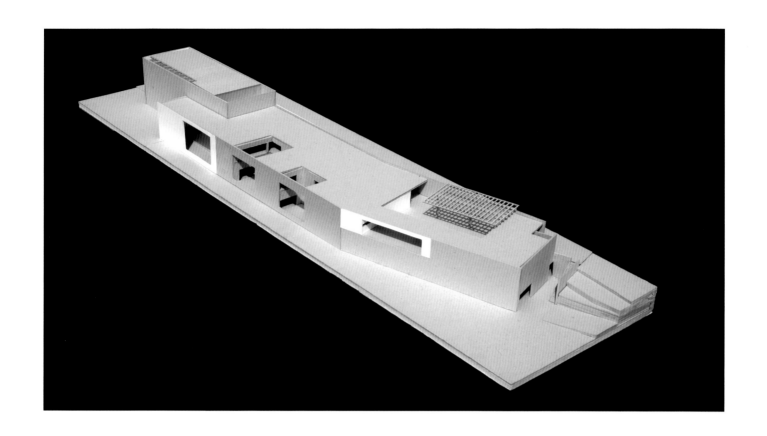

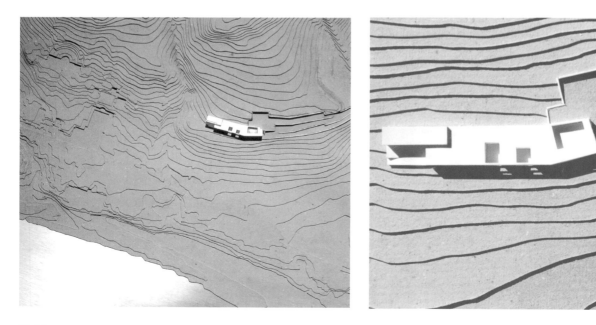

Models

Location maps

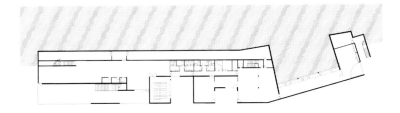

First floor

Second floor

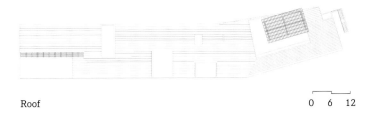

Roof

0   6   12

Elevation

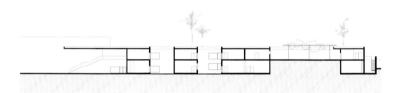

Sections

■ Guillermo Vázquez Consuegra graduated in Architecture from the Seville School of Architecture since 1972. He was the projects professor until 1987 and has been a guest lecturer at various foreign universities, in Buenos Aires, Lausanne, Venice and Bologna. He has taken part in numerous national and international exhibitions, including the Venice Biennale (1980 and 2004). His works and projects have been published in Spanish and foreign journals and he has participated in seminars and conferences in Europe, South America and the US. He has taken home prizes from Spain and abroad and his works include various social-housing buildings in Seville, Madrid and Rota, the Expo 92 Sailing Pavilion and the National Museum of Maritime Archeology in Cartagena.

## G. Vázquez Consuegra

# Steven Holl Architects

## Higgins Hall Center Section Brooklyn, NY, USA

■ The new building connects the north and south wings of Higgens Hall, a historical New York building that is home to the Pratt Institute School of Architecture. The Center Section building covers an area of more than 21,000 sq ft and features various levels and facilities including a foyer, gallery, terrace, auditorium, digital research center, two classrooms and various architectural studios. For this building, the architects used an elemental structure of concrete covered in thick glass. The aim was to create a strong visual contrast with the cross-buildings, which have masonry facades. This helped the designers establish a groundbreaking approach to the problem of inserting new buildings into a preexisting architectural context.

© Paul Warchol

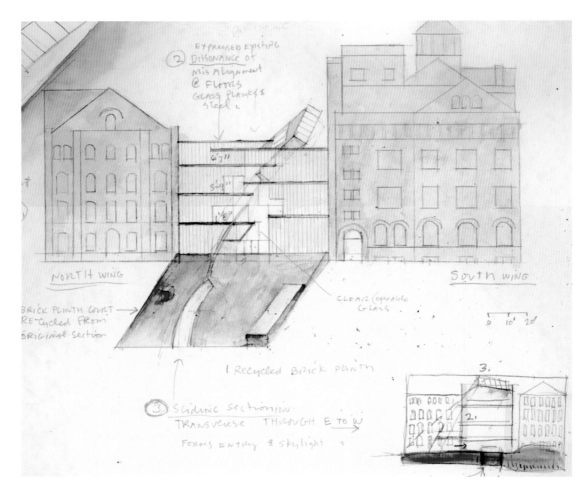

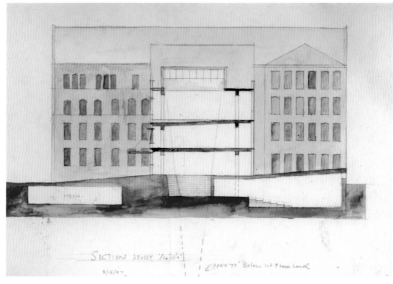

Sketches

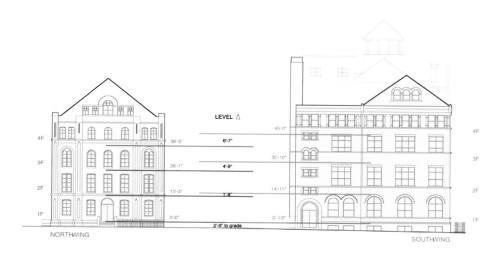

Diagram of the level difference between the existing buildings

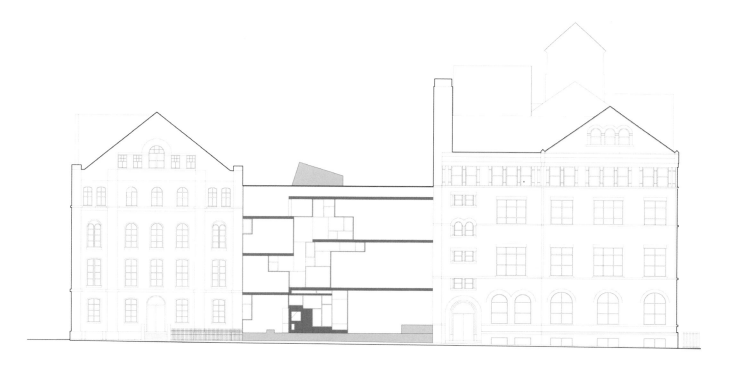

Elevation

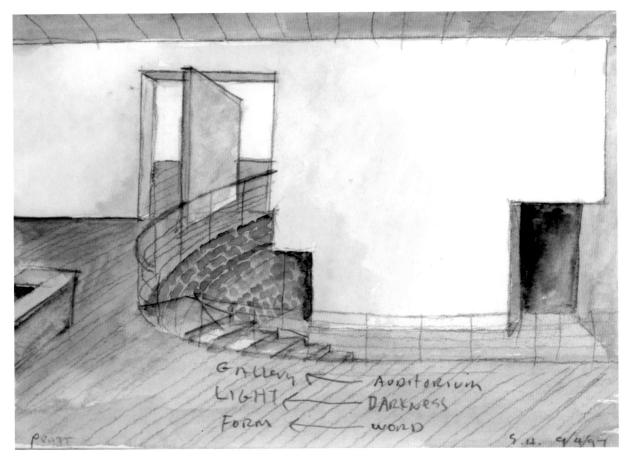

GALLERY ← AUDITORIUM
LIGHT ← DARKNESS
FORM ← WORD

PRATT                                    S.H. 4/4/97

Sketches

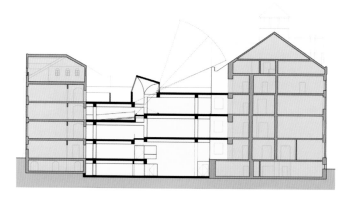

Longitudinal section

Cross-section

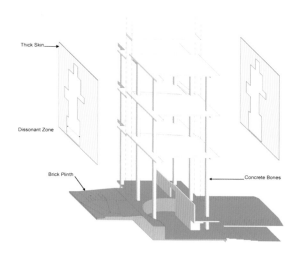

Isometric diagram

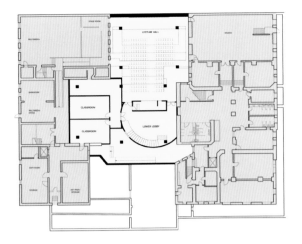

Basement

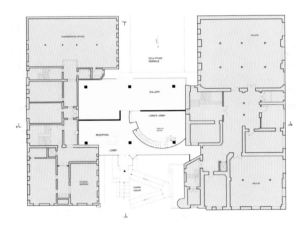

First floor

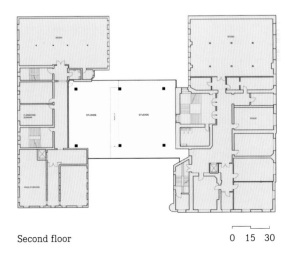

Second floor

0  15  30

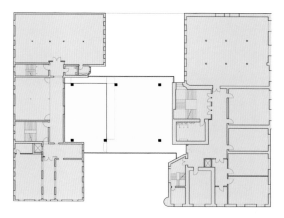

Third floor

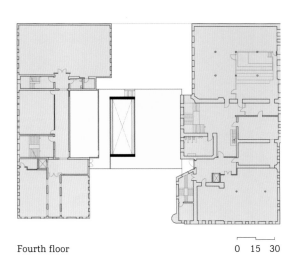

Fourth floor

0   15   30

■ Steven Holl was born in Bremerton, Washington in 1947. He graduated from the University of Washington and went on to study architecture in Rome in 1970. In 1976 he founded Steven Holl Architects in New York, a studio which today has offices in New York and Beijing and 49 people on staff. The company's work has been published and exhibited on many occasions and received numerous awards. He is considered one of America's premier architects and his work is recognized for its ability to combine space and light with a great sensitivity for context.

## Steven Holl Architects

# Snøhetta AS

# Oslo Opera House Oslo, Norway

■ The Oslo Opera House is the first element of transformation in this part of the city. The public tender specified various elements essential to the design: the 'wave wall', symbolizing a threshold between water and earth; a second element the architects defined as the 'factory', i.e., a space that covers the opera house facilities, and finally the 'carpet', or roof – a response to demand for a monumental public space. The materials used play a vital role in the final result: glass, white marble for the roof, wood for the wave wall and metal for the factory. The result is a building characterized by its marked horizontal nature and whose roof forms a large public space implemented in the landscape of the city and the fjord.

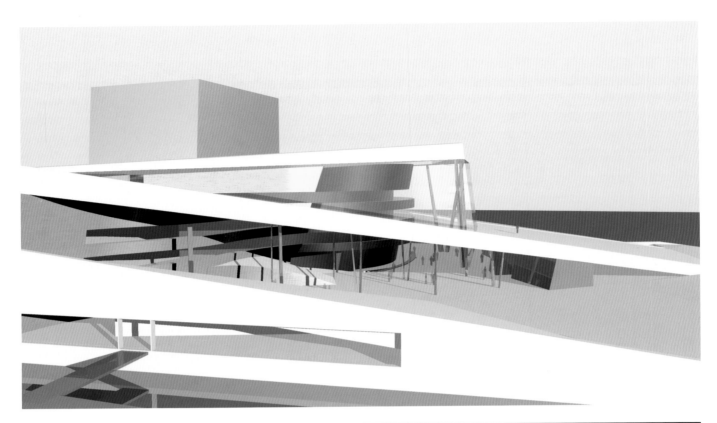

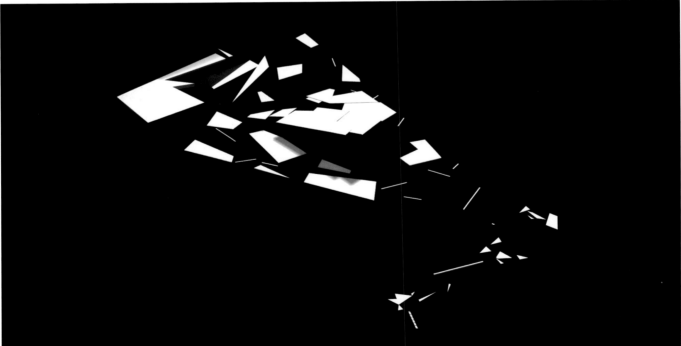

Renderings

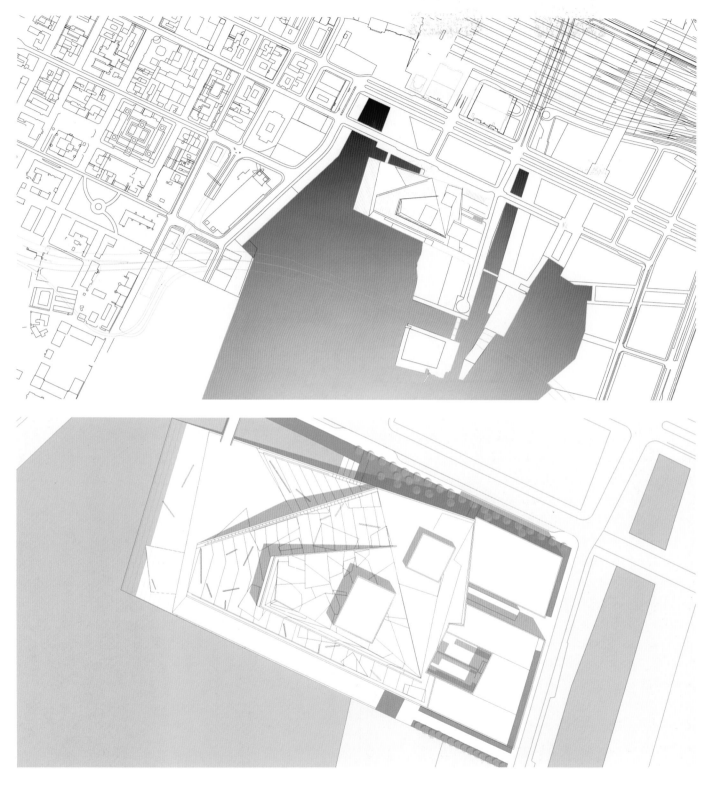

Location maps

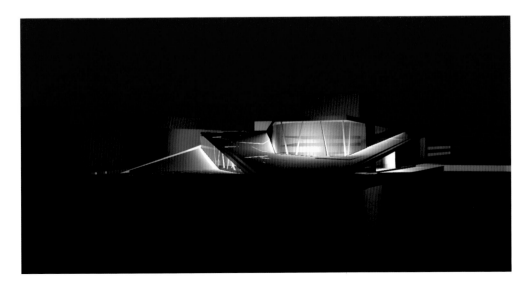

Renderings

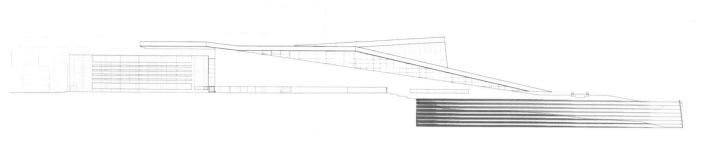

North elevation

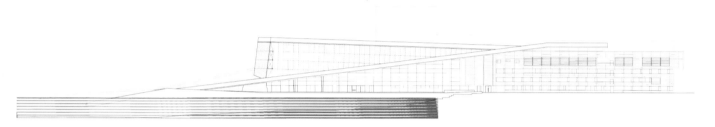

South elevation

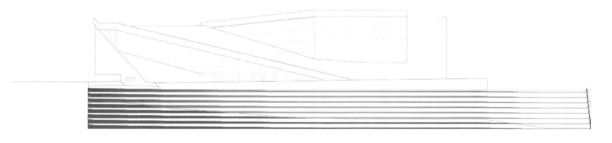

West elevation

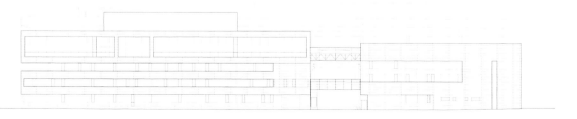

East elevation

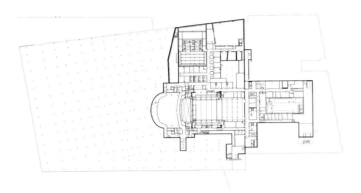

Basement

First floor

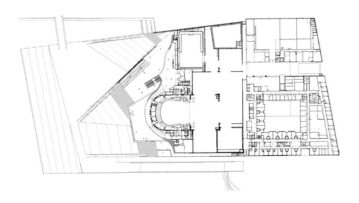

Second floor

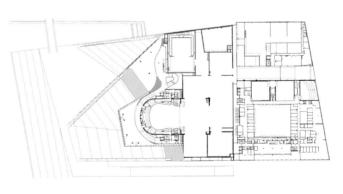

Third floor

0   15   30

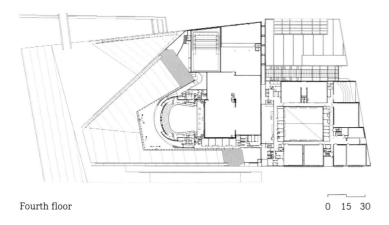

Fourth floor

0   15   30

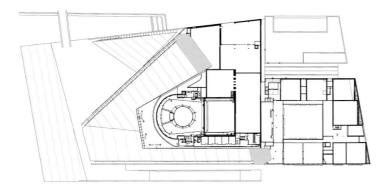

Fifth floor

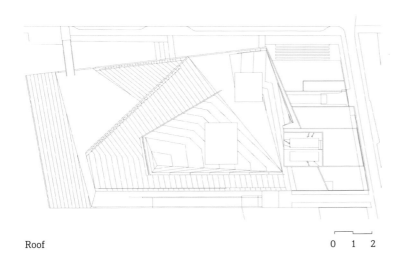

Roof

0   1   2

■ Snøhetta AS was founded in Norway in 1989 and has offices in Oslo and New York. It is a studio that integrates architecture, interior design and landscape design, where the staff members share spaces. Staff are trained by an international team of professionals with experience in the US and Middle East, although work is done in an atmosphere of contemporary European design. More than 15 years' design and building experience and various culture-related projects have given the studio a formidable reputation and seen it scoop important architectural awards such as the Aga Khan.

## Snøhetta AS

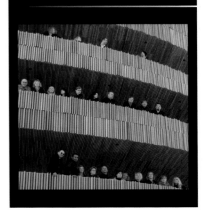

# Álvaro Siza

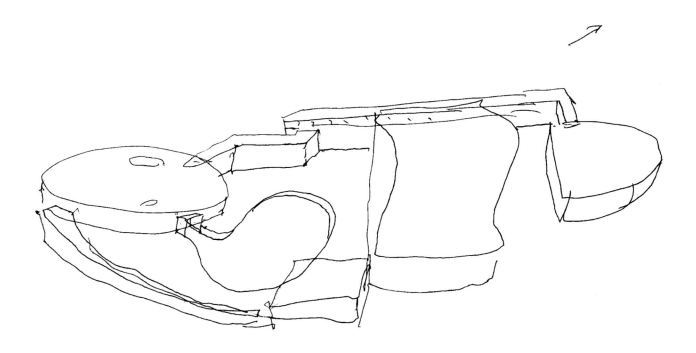

## Swimming pool in Cornellà de Llobregat Cornellà de Llobregat, Spain

■ This sports facility, of sinuous and elegant forms, is composed of three principal spaces: a multisport pavilion that seats 2,500 people; an aquatic area and a gym. Access to the facility is via a gentle slope in the north-east and south-east areas, delimited by the pavilion and a longitudinal volume around which entry to the facility is organized. The aquatic area is composed of two swimming pools: indoors and outdoors, which communicate so it is not necessary to get out of the water to move from one to the other. The gym has an independent entrance and shares the dressing rooms and swimming-pool facilities. This sports complex has given the city of Cornellà de Llobregat, close to Barcelona, a new and modern public space.

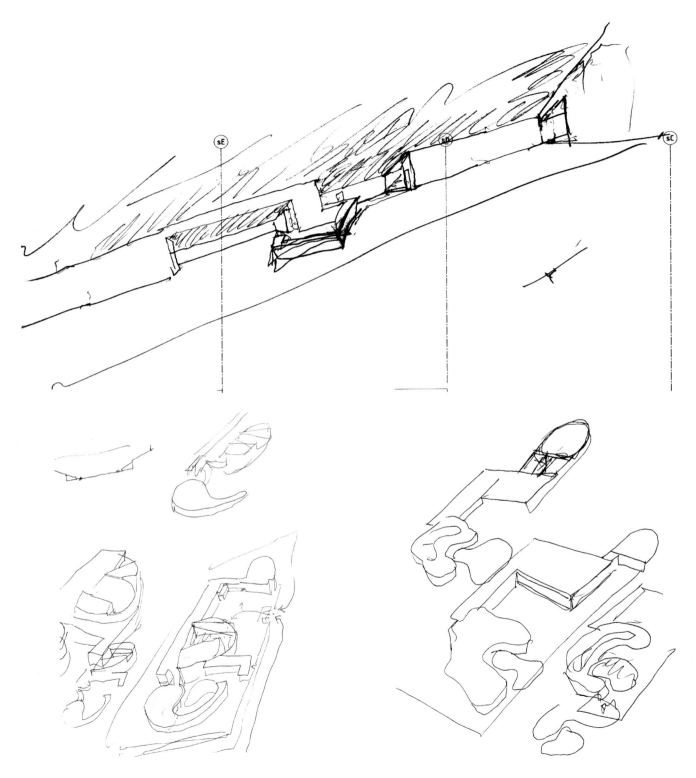

Sketches

Sketch

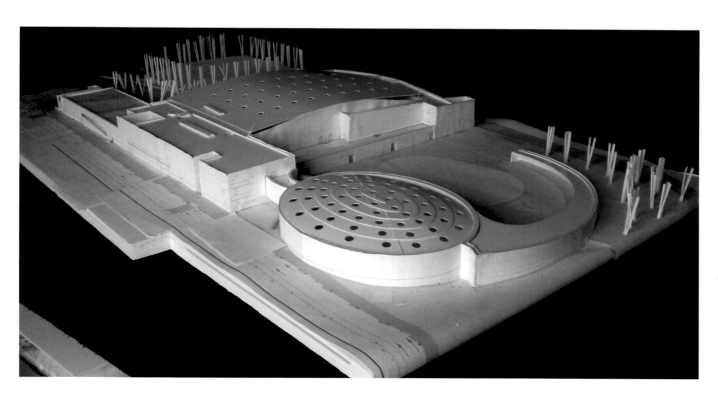

Model

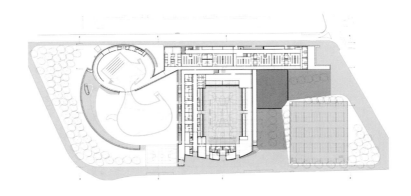

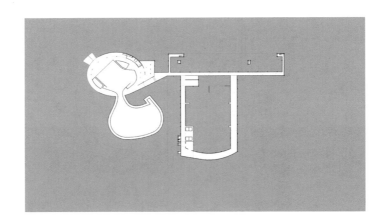

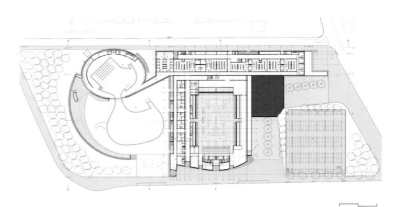

Floor plans

0  20  40

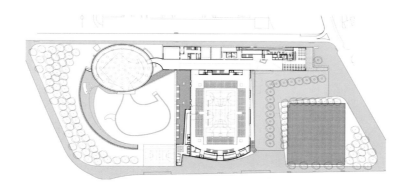

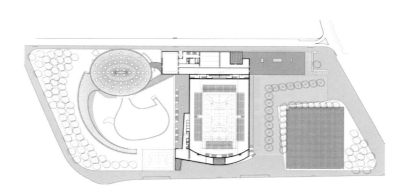

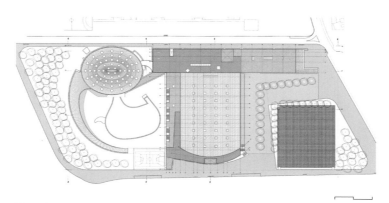

Floor plans

0  20  40

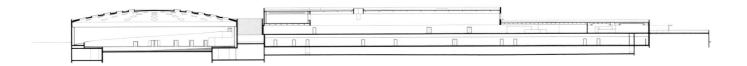

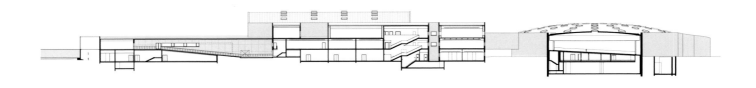

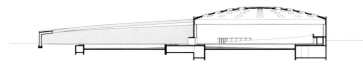

Sections

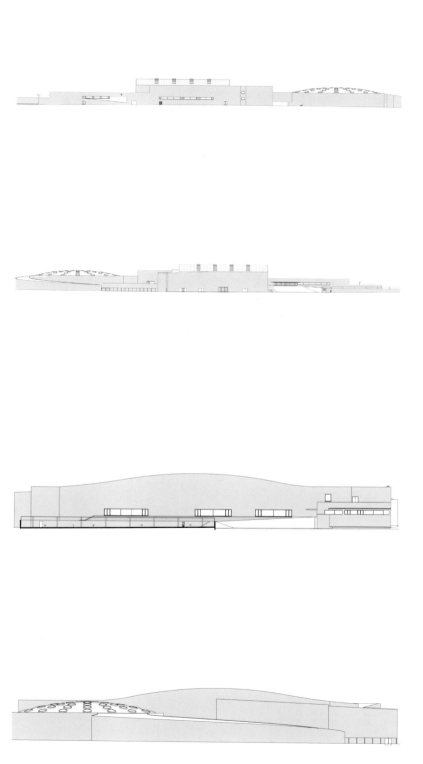

Elevations

Álvaro Joaquim de Melo Siza was born in Matosinhos in 1933. He studied architecture at the Porto School of Fine Arts between 1949 and 1955, although his first built work dates from 1954. He has been a guest lecturer at leading universities such as the Lausanne Polytechnic, the University of Pennsylvania and the Los Andes School in Bogota. He works as a professor in Porto and is a member of the American Academy of Arts and Sciences, an honorary member of the Royal Institute of British Architects and a member of the European Academy of Arts and Science. He is furthermore an honorary doctor of more than 12 universities.

## Álvaro Siza

# Antonio Galiano, Rafael Landete

## Alicante New Port Access Alicante, Spain

■ The project for the new port access to the city began with an analysis of the port activities involved and the needs that had to be covered. The design includes two concepts, apparently contradictory, which respond to the port's current requirements: integration and exclusion. On the one hand, the aim was to integrate the space within the city architecture, as the port has always been of vital importance to Alicante's development. However, every port needs security measures, so it was also necessary to restrict the access. The new building spans the width of the end of one of the most important avenues in town. The passage is limited by architectural elements that recall ancient entry gates.

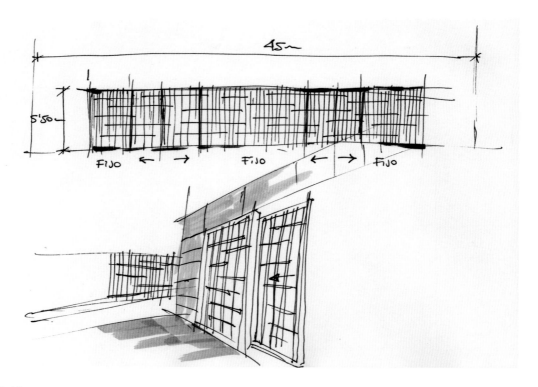

Sketches

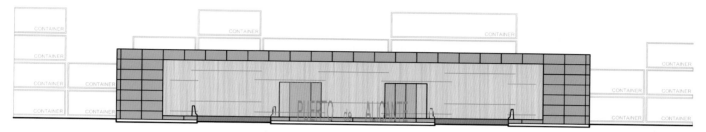

Closed northern elevation

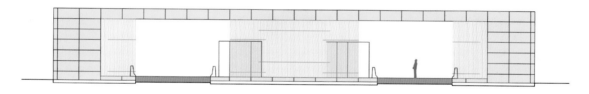

Open southern elevation

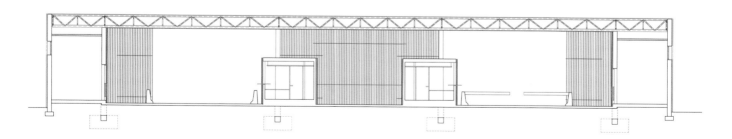

Longitudinal section

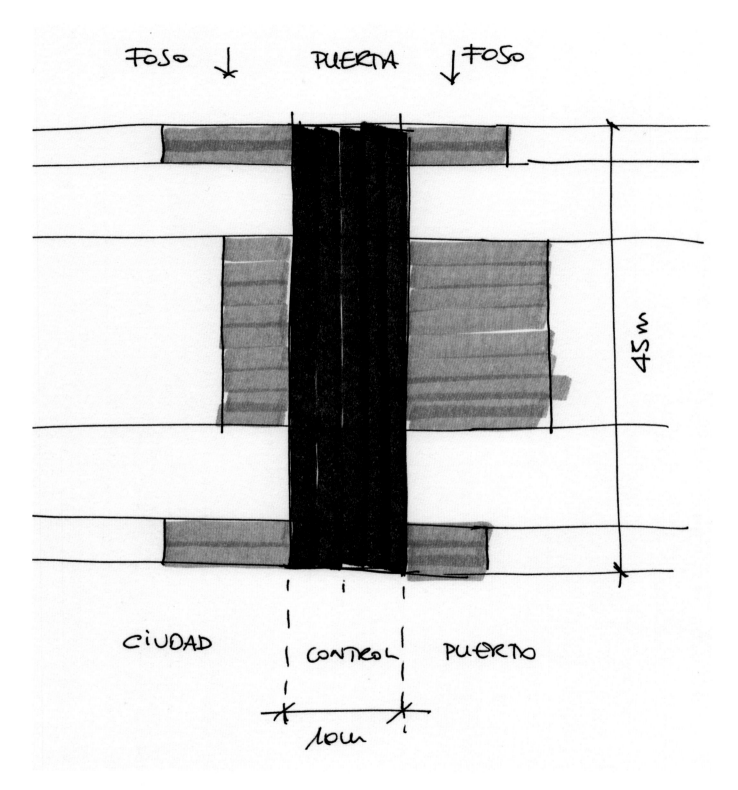

FOSO PUERTA FOSO

45m

CIUDAD CONTROL PUERTO

10m

Location map

■ Antonio Galiano Garrigós was born in Orihuela (Alicante) in 1974. A graduate of the Valencia School of Architecture, he set up his own studio in the year 2000 in conjunction with Rafael Landete, with whom he worked until 2005. He is a professor of architecture at the University of Alicante. Rafael Landete was born in Alcoy and presently works in Alicante. He defines himself as a defender of architecture at the service of the people. The studio Galiano Garrigós Arquitectos is formed of young professionals who specialize in the development of singular buildings for different uses.

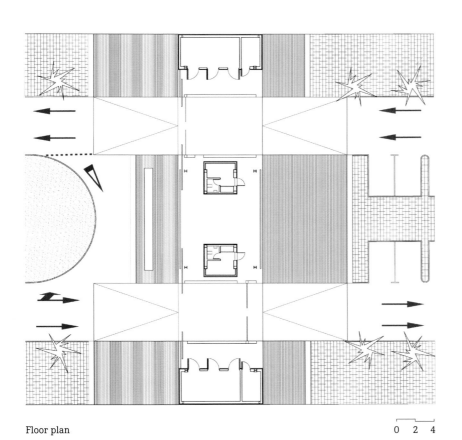

Floor plan

0  2  4

## Antonio Galiano, Rafael Landete

# Paulo David

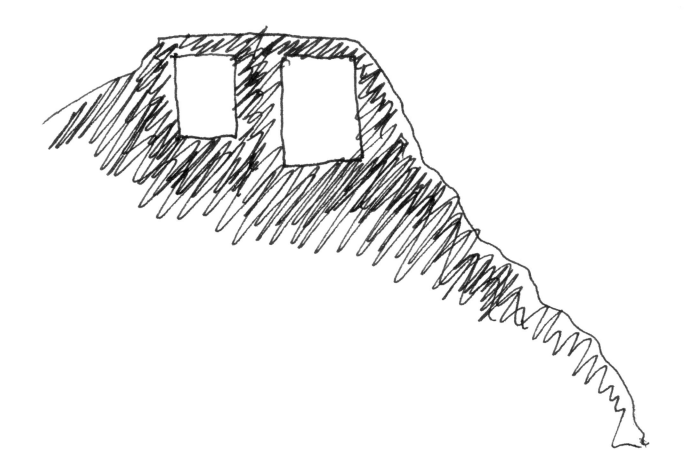

## Casa das Mudas Arts Center Calheta, Madeira, Portugal

■ The Casa das Mudas Arts Center is strategically located on a steep cliff that projects over the Atlantic Ocean. The original concept was for the building to act only as a landscape framework. The result is a group of sculptural volumes formed by an abstract geometry that merges with nature. The nucleus was developed along a north-south axis whose length was adapted to the limits of the terrain. The main entrance is via a courtyard where all the design functions are distributed independently, although they are interrelated on lower levels. The building has a black basalt basis and references the volcanic nature of the environment. Its color and texture generate an organic continuity between building, landscape and nature.

157

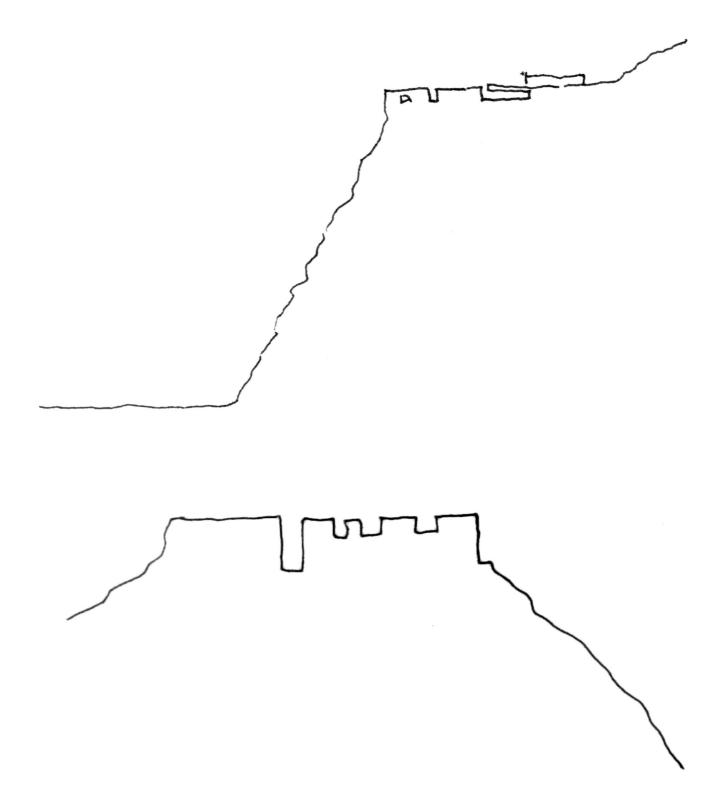

Sketches

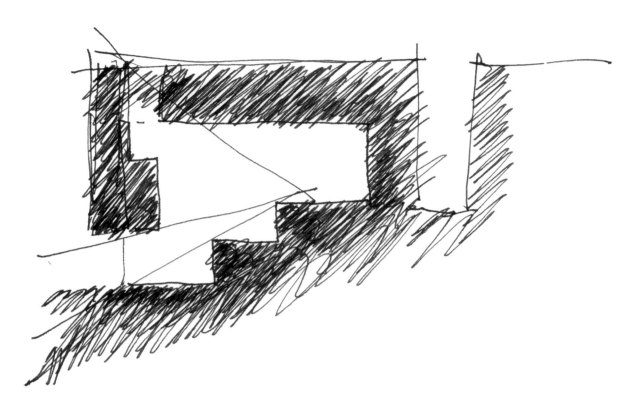

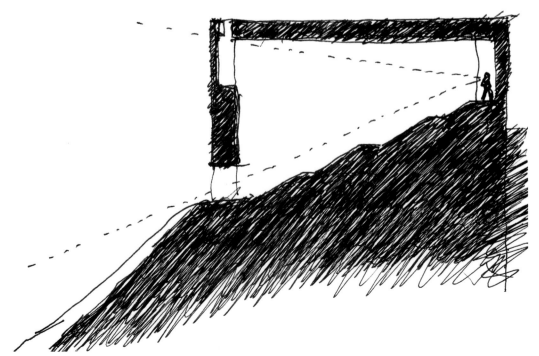

Sketches

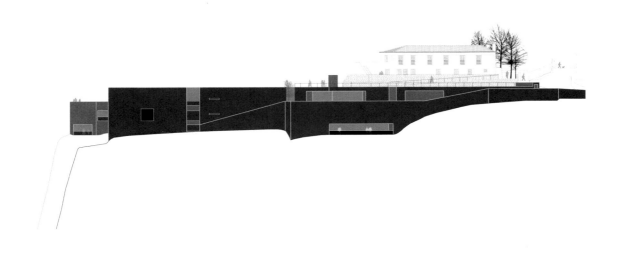

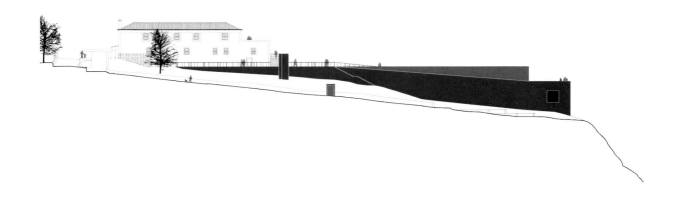

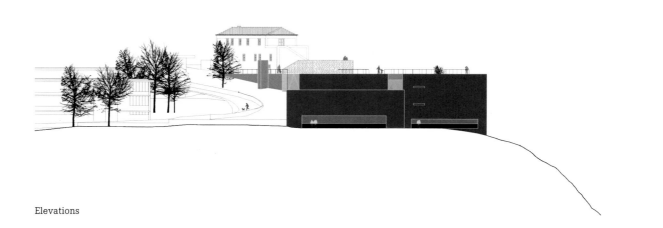

Elevations

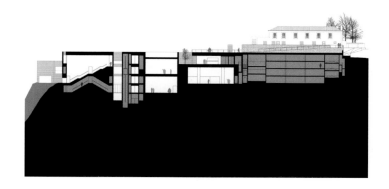

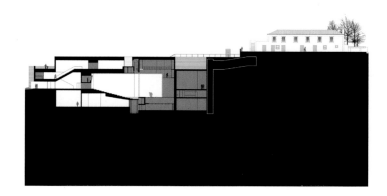

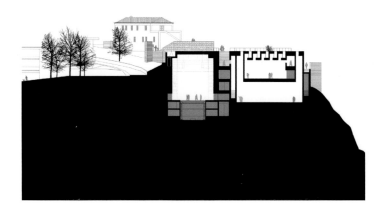

Sections

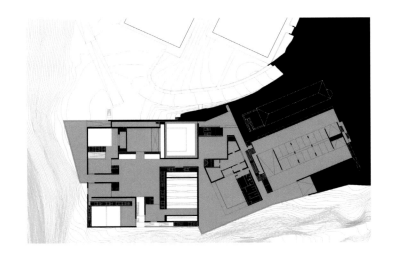

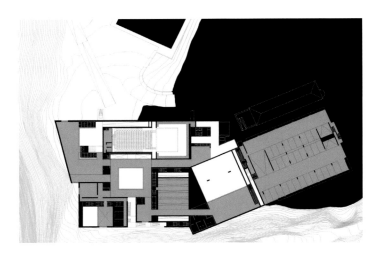

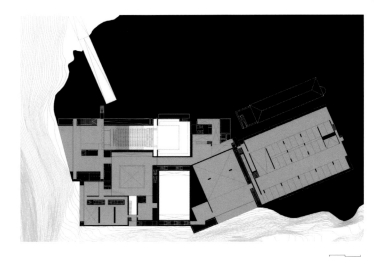

Floor plans

0  6  12

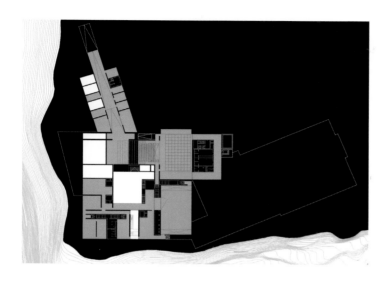

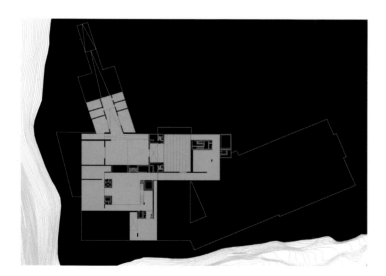

Floor plans

0  6  12

■ Paulo David was born in Funchal in 1959. He graduated from the Faculty of Architecture at the Technical University of Lisbon in 1989. Before setting up on his own, he worked for the Gonçalo Byrne studio between 1988 and 1996 and the João Luís Carrilho da Graça studio in 1989. He was also a consultant for Funchal City Council and a guest lecturer at the University of Madeira's School of Art and Design between 2001 and 2004 and its Faculty of Civil Engineering in 2006 and 2007. He has won numerous architecture awards for Casa das Mudas, including the Mies van der Rohe in 2005. His work has been published in several books and specialist magazines.

## Paulo David

# G. Vázquez Consuegra

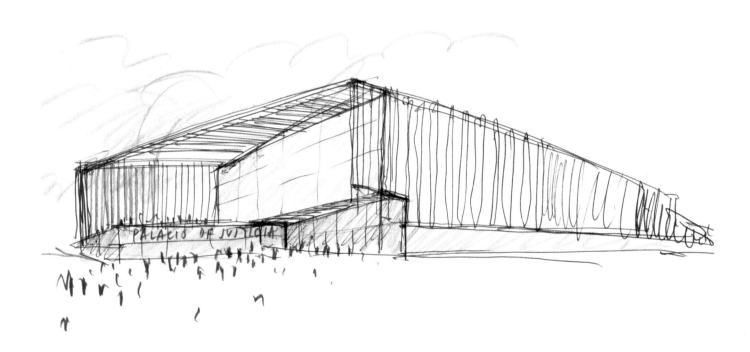

## **Ciudad Real Courts** Ciudad Real, Spain

■ The new court building is located on an estate outside the historical city and surrounded by industrial estates, low-density housing and emerging residential buildings. The project involved the construction of a U-shaped building that would enable the location of a complex program and facilitate the creation of an open space. A triangular space covered by a glass roof forms a square that provides access to the building. Between the two parallel pieces is the foyer, a large area in line with the physical and public dimensions of the building. This space has extensive walkways that act as nexuses between the two blocks. This generates a bright and transparent space that permits the natural lighting of the interiors.

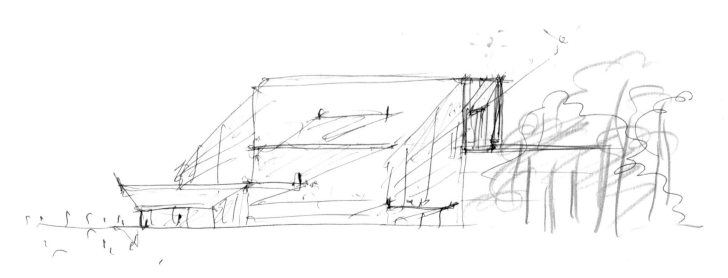

Sketches

Sketches

167

Sketch

Rendering

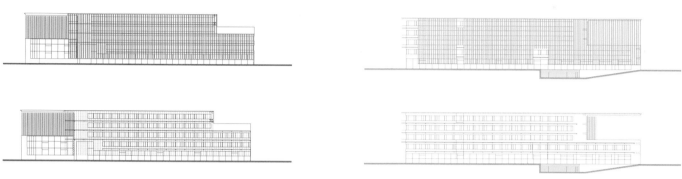

Elevations

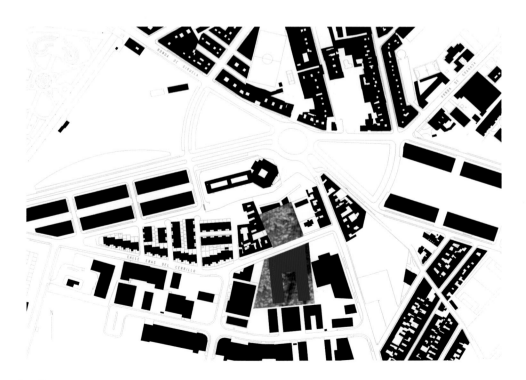

Location map

Basement floor

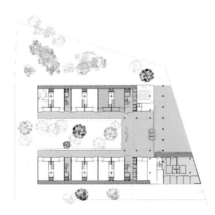

First floor

Second floor

0  10  20

Third floor

Fourth floor

0  10  20

■ Guillermo Vázquez Consuegra graduated in Architecture from the Seville School of Architecture since 1972. He was the projects professor until 1987 and has been a guest lecturer at various foreign universities, in Buenos Aires, Lausanne, Venice and Bologna. He has taken part in numerous national and international exhibitions, including the Venice Biennale (1980 and 2004). His works and projects have been published in Spanish and foreign journals and he has participated in seminars and conferences in Europe, South America and the US. He has taken home prizes from Spain and abroad and his works include various social-housing buildings in Seville, Madrid and Rota, the Expo 92 Sailing Pavilion and the National Museum of Maritime Archeology in Cartagena.

## G. Vázquez Consuegra

# Mitchell Taylor Workshop

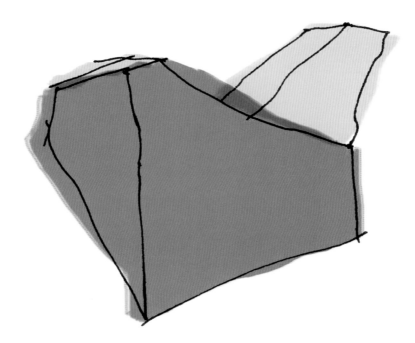

## Room 13 Bristol, United Kingdom

■ Room 13 is a space democratically administered by the students of the school who commissioned the project. Hareclive Primary School appointed the architects to design a space that would function as a classroom and art room. It would substitute the art room of the existing school and provide a space to exhibit the students' artistic creations. Room 13 is a large area lit by skylights, although the interior can be divided into various compartments to facilitate its use as a classroom and community area. The building materials are cheap and hardy: concrete blocks for three of the four exterior walls, glass for the north façade and a roof made from Sarnafil. Storage areas were built inside for material and equipment.

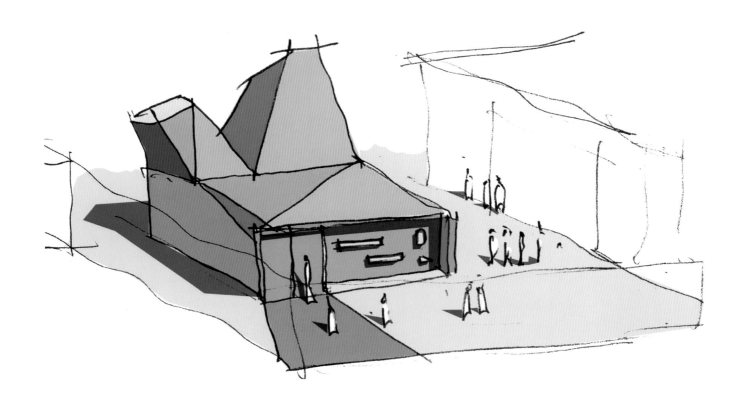

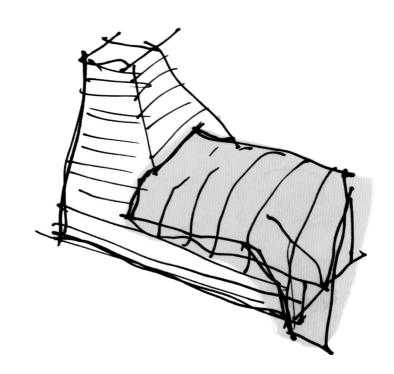

Sketches

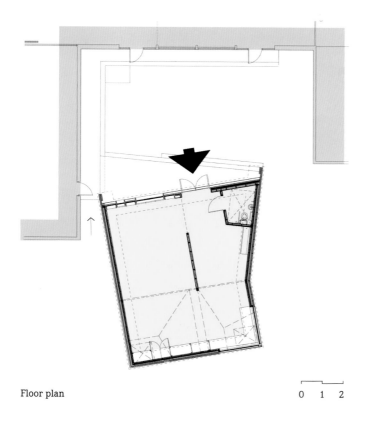

Floor plan

0   1   2

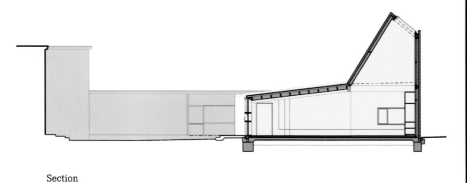

Section

■ The studio formed by Piers Taylor and Rob Mitchell features a young and progressive team that has picked up numerous awards. Sustainable architecture and works that not only mix with the environment but connect with a site via differences is a fundamental principle of their professional practice. The projects the studio has made have scooped many awards and been published on numerous occasions. However, the architects stress that what concerns them most is that their buildings result from a careful and detailed analysis of the requirements of each and every case.

**Mitchell Taylor Workshop**

# Rafael Viñoly Architects

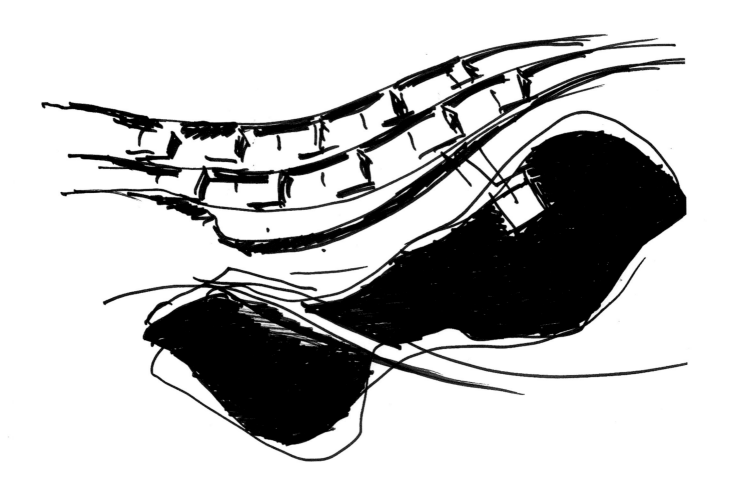

# Howard Hughes Medical Institute Ashburn, VA, USA

■ The Howard Hughes Medical Institute (HHMI) decided to take advantage of the opportunity for expansion to put out a tender for the construction of a modern research campus equipped with the latest technology. Rafael Viñoly Architects' design consists of various undulating buildings set on terraces created on a gently sloping hillside. The different levels cover all the project elements: common areas, laboratories, meeting and conference rooms, offices, apartments and a hotel. Interaction between building and landscape is another strong point of the project. In the words of the architect, the landscape is the building: it creates a counterpoint between sustainable technology and nature. A natural design adapted to the environment which conceals a construction of great technical complexity.

© Paul Fetters

# A "LANDSCAPE" BUILDING

## (NOT a MEGASTRUCTURE)

● <u>The slope</u>

● <u>A Terraced Garden</u>

Sketch

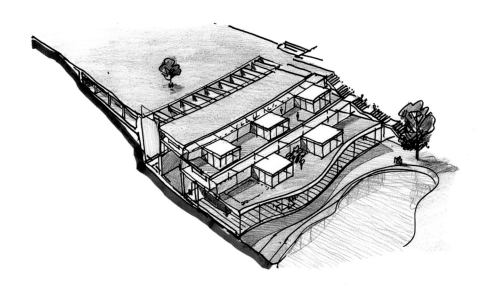

Sketches

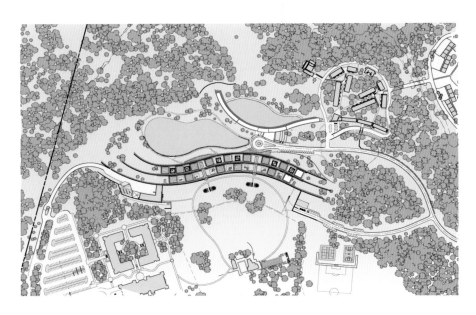

Location map

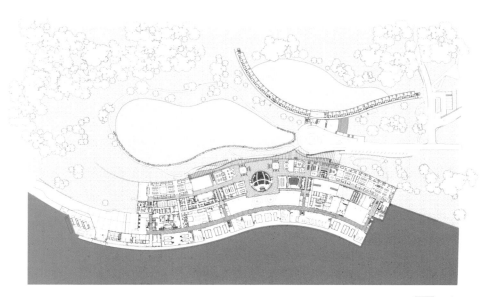

Floor plan

0  15  30

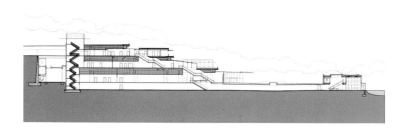

Sections

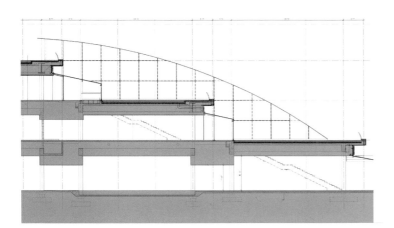

Detail of a roof section

■ Rafael Viñoly was born in Uruguay in 1944 and founded his first architectural studio at the age of 20. Throughout the 45-plus years he has been working in the USA, Argentina, Europe, the Middle East and Asia he has followed the belief that architecture's essential responsibility is to emphasize its public dimension. He has focused on maximizing the opportunity that public investment gives each project. As well as his professional dedication and success in numerous tenders, Rafael Viñoly has taken home important awards, been published in a great many specialist publications and is publicly renowned as an expert conference speaker.

## Rafael Viñoly Architects

# Vidal y Asociados Arquitectos, Araujo-Berned Arquitectos (collaborators)

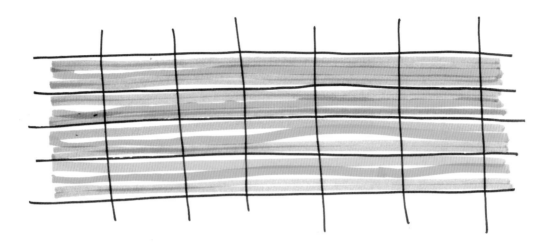

# Vallecas Hospital Vallecas, Spain

■ The architect Luis Vidal has specialized in public buildings. His extensive experience on large-scale projects, such as the new Saragossa Airport terminal, was applied to the construction of this 968,751 sq ft hospital. Vallecas Hospital, built in conjunction with Araújo Berned Arquitectos, is a three-storey building with significant flexibility: its design permits it to grow vertically and horizontally. The backbone of the building is a corridor that branches off into different rooms. The various medical services are distributed in areas identified by different colors (blue, yellow, red, green, orange and violet), facilitating orientation. Sustainable architecture shores up a truly 21st-century construction conceived to guarantee comfort and maximize patient quality of life.

© Miguel de Guzmán

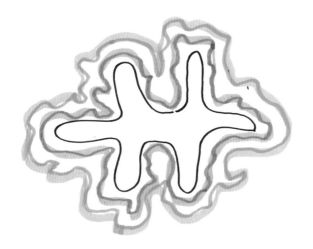

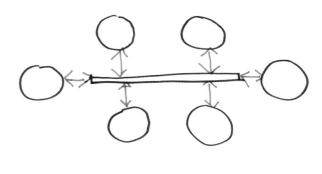

Sketches

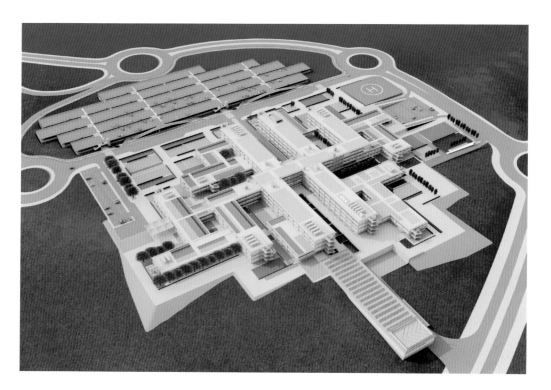

Rendering

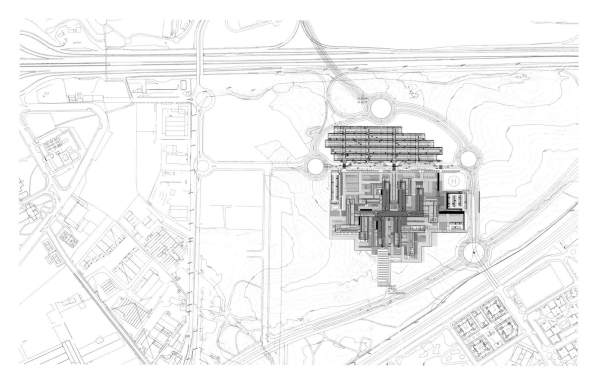

Location map

Rendering

Renderings

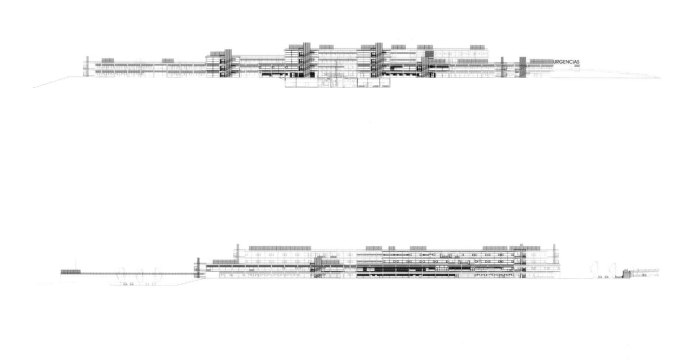

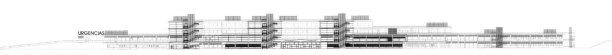

Elevations

Longitudinal sections

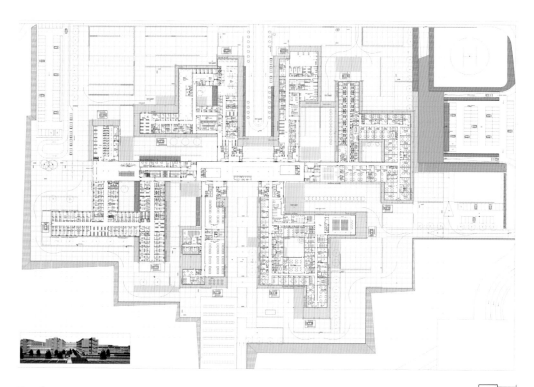

First floor

0  10  20

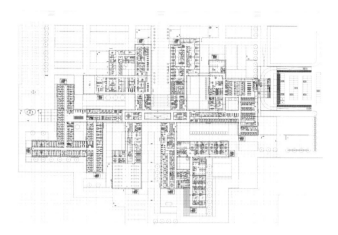

Second floor

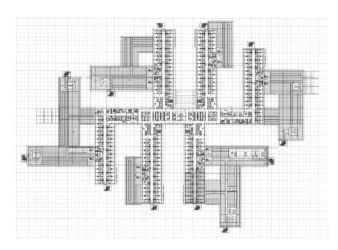

Third floor

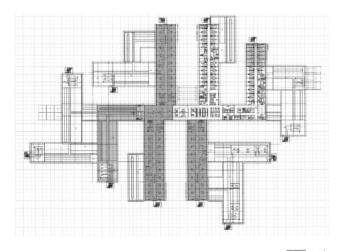

Fourth floor

0   20   40

■ Vidal y Asociados Arquitectos was founded in 2004 thanks to the ground-breaking vision of Luis Vidal and the commitment of his group of young professionals. Their goal is to create quality sustainable architecture and provide creative responses to contemporary architectural problems. Luis Vidal, who studied at the University of Greenwich and is a member of the Royal Institute of British Architects, is responsible for projects such as Warsaw International Airport and the Sergi Arola restaurant in the Reina Sofía Museum, and his studio has worked with the Richard Rogers Partnership on various projects in Spain.

## Vidal y Asociados Arquitectos

# Directory

Patel Taylor
53 Rawstorne Street
EC1V 7NQ London, United Kingdom
Tel. +44 20 7278 2323
Fax +44 20 7278 6242
pta@pateltaylor.co.uk
www.pateltaylor.co.uk

Lehrer Architects
2140 Hyperion Ave
Los Angeles, CA 90027-4708, USA
Tel. +1 323 664 4747
Fax +1 323 664 3566
architect@lehrerarchitects.com
www.lehrerarchitects.com

Abeijón Fernández
Juan Florez 118, 1º
15005 La Coruña, Spain
Tel. +34 981 153 544
Fax +34 881 925 229
www.abeijon-fernandez.com

Gatermann + Schossig
Richartzstrasse 10
50667 Cologne, Germany
Tel. +49 (0) 221 925821 0
Fax +49 (0) 221 925821 70
info@gatermann-schossig.de
www.gatermann-schossig.de

Miguel Ángel Roca
Av. Poeta Lugones, 464
5000 Córboba, Argentina
Tel. +54 351 4684 186
Fax +54 351 4699 346
info@miguelangelroca.com
www.miguelangelroca.com

EMBT – Enric Miralles, Benedetta Tagliabue
Passatge de la Pau, 10 bis, pral.
08002 Barcelona, Spain
Tel. +34 934 125 342
Fax +34 934 123 718
info@mirallestagliabue.com
www.mirallestagliabue.com

Satoshi Okada Architects
16-12-302/303 Tomihisha
Shinjuku, Tokyo 162-0067, Japan
Tel. +81 3 3355 0646
Fax +81 3 3355 1658
mail@okada-archi.com
www.okada-archi.com

Steven Holl Architects
450 West 31st Street, 11th floor
New York, NY 10001, USA
Tel. +1 212 629 7262
Fax +1 212 629 7312
nyc@stevenholl.com
www.stevenholl.com

RMJM HK
33rd floor Grand Millenium Plaza, Cosco Tower
183 Queen's Road Central, Hong Kong
Tel. +852 2548 1698
Fax +852 2547 6386
www.rmjm.com

Elisabet Faura & Gerard Veciana/Arteks Arquitectura
Unió, 1, 1º A
AD500 Andorra La Vella, Andorra
Tel. +376 805 225
Fax +376 823 272
info@arteks.ad
www.arteksarquitectura.com

Esther Pascal Riera
Josep Viladomat, 38, esc. A, 6º 2ª
AD700 Escaldes, Andorra
Tel. +376 860 634
epascal@andorra.ad


Ona Arquitectes
Montmany, 27, local
08012 Barcelona, Spain
Tel. +34 934 151 931
Fax +34 932 136 587
ona@onaarquitectes.com
www.onaarquitectes.com


Vázquez Consuegra
Laraña, 6
41003 Seville, Spain
Tel. +34 954 213 590
Fax +34 954 219 673
estudio@vazquezconsuegra.com
www.vazquezconsuegra.com


Snøhetta AS
Skur 39, Vippetangen
0150 Oslo, Norway
Tel. +47 24 15 60 60
Fax +47 24 15 60 61
contact@snoarc.no
www.snoarc.no


Álvaro Siza
Rua Aleixo 53, 2nd floor
4150-043 Oporto, Portugal
Tel. +351 22 616 7270
Fax +351 22 616 7279
siza@mail.telepac.pt


Galiano Garrigós Arquitectos
San Francisco 27, 1º
03001 Alicante, Spain
Tel./Fax +34 965 214 639
estudio@galianogarrigos.com
www.galianogarrigos.com


Paulo David
Rua da Carreira 73, 5th floor
9000 042 Funchal, Madeira, Portugal
Tel. +351 291 281 840
Fax +351 291 281 852
pd.arq@mail.telepac.pt


Mitchell Taylor Workshop
Wharf Studio, Widcombe Hill
BA2 6AA Bath, United Kingdom
Tel./Fax +44 1225 789033
studio@mitchelltaylorworkshop.co.uk
www.mitchelltaylorworkshop.co.uk


Rafael Viñoly Architects
50 Vandam Street
New York, NY 10013, USA
Tel. +1 212 924 50 60
Fax +1 212 924 58 58
info@rvapc.com
www.rvapc.com


Vidal y Asociados Arquitectos
Velázquez, 78
28001 Madrid, Spain
Tel. +34 913 593 900
Fax +34 913 599 300
info@luisvidal.com
www.luisvidal.com